CHAMBERS

GUIDE TO PUNCTUATION

edited by
Kay Cullen

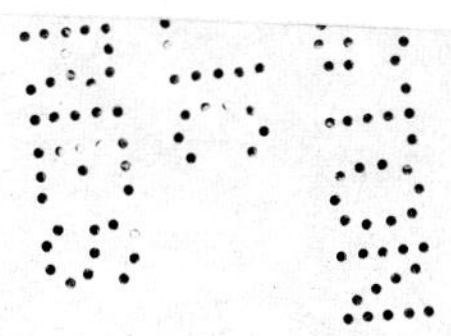

CHAMBERS

CHAMBERS
An imprint of Chambers Harrap Publishers Ltd
7 Hopetoun Crescent
Edinburgh EH7 4AY

A CIP catalogue record for this book is available from the British Library.

We have made every effort to mark as such all words which we believe to be trademarks.
We should also like to make it clear that the presence of a word in this book, whether marked or unmarked, in no way affects its legal status as a trademark.

ISBN 0550 14140 5

The British National Corpus is a collaborative initiative carried out by Oxford University Press, Longman, Chambers Harrap, Oxford University Computing Services, Lancaster University's Unit for Computer Research in the English Language, and the British Library. The project received funding from the UK department of Trade and Industry and the Science and Engineering Research Council, and was supported by additional research grants from the British Academy and the British Library.

Series editor:
Penny Hands

Typeset by Chambers Harrap Publishers Ltd
Printed and bound in Great Britain by
Cox & Wyman Ltd, Reading, Berkshire

Contents

Introduction	v
The full stop	1
The question mark	6
The exclamation mark	9
The apostrophe	12
The comma	17
The colon	28
The semicolon	31
Quotation marks	34
Brackets	41
Dashes and slashes	46
The hyphen	51
Capital letters	56
Abbreviations	59
Diacritics and accents	64
Numbers, fractions and dates	67
Miscellaneous	71
American style	75
Exercises	78
Solutions to exercises	83
Index	87

Introduction

What is punctuation and why is it important?

Punctuation is the system of non-alphabetical symbols that we use in writing to group words together, and to separate words and groups of words from each other.

To answer the second part of the question, try reading the following paragraph:

> its Anne Peter Ive come to take you home she said gently he made no outward sign that he had heard or understood her he was sitting hunched up in the corner hugging his knees which were drawn up to his chest eyes tightly closed and making a sound like an animal in pain he went on rocking himself slowly backwards and forwards backwards and forwards

Clearly then, punctuation makes writing and printing easier to read. It is an aid to comprehension on two levels: it gives the reader information about how the text might be read aloud using appropriate pauses and intonation; and, more importantly, it shows how words relate to each other, marking off elements in the broader grammatical structure.

This book deals with all the major punctuation marks in turn so that readers who want to explore the subject fully can familiarize themselves with the rules and conventions that apply to each. This will permit them to build on their knowledge as they move from one chapter to the next. The structure of the book makes it equally easy to dip into, if information about the proper use of a particular punctuation mark, such as the comma, the semicolon, or the colon, is needed.

In each chapter, there are lots of examples that illustrate clearly how a particular punctuation mark should or should not be used.

The symbol ✓ before an example is the indicator of correct use, and the symbol ✗ identifies examples where punctuation has been used incorrectly.

Variations in style are discussed throughout the book. For example, you can sometimes choose to use or to omit a mark in a particular context without affecting the sense. Where a punctuation mark is not considered to be obligatory, this is explained in detail. However, it is important to remember that when there is such a choice, the method you adopt should be consistent throughout a piece of writing. Perhaps the most obvious variation in punctuation style that you are likely to encounter is between British and American texts. The British are much more likely to use an 'open' system: that is, to use fewer punctuation marks than would be used in a comparable American text. These differences are summarized in Chapter 17.

The final chapter of the book contains a series of short exercises, should readers choose to practise what they have learned in previous chapters.

We hope that you will find that reading and using this book will remove any uncertainty you might have had about your use of punctuation, and, as a result, you are confident that your writing is clearer and more accurate.

Other guides in the same series include *Guide to Common Errors*, *Guide to Effective Grammar*, and *Guide to Letter Writing*.

1

The full stop

The **full stop** (.) is also known as a **period** or a **full point**.

The full stop as a sentence marker

The main use of the full stop is as a sentence marker. Most people are aware of the rule that a sentence should start with a capital letter and, when it is not a question or an exclamation, should end with a full stop. Thus, the full stop is the correct punctuation mark to use in sentences that express complete statements, as in the following examples:

> Our flight is due to leave at 6 o'clock.
>
> The new edition of our best-selling dictionary is available in the shops now.

In a continuous block of text, each sentence is ended with a full stop and the first letter of the next sentence starts with a capital letter. There should be no space between the full stop and the last letter of each sentence.

Notice the use of full stops in the following extract from the introduction to *Chambers 21st Century Dictionary*:

> A major challenge in the compilation of any English dictionary lies in the need to explain how words are used in conjunction with other words; after all, we speak and write phrases and sentences, and meanings emerge from the interaction of words rather than merely from the individual words themselves. Chambers dictionaries are justly famous for their excellence in exemplifying and explaining the idiomatic aspects of language. In this dictionary, we go still further in this process, and include phrasal verbs in this generous treatment, by explaining idioms and phrases in their typical surroundings (or *collocation*). This will be especially noticeable in highly functional and productive words such as *get* and *turn*, which often have little meaning in themselves and

derive their meaning from the words that accompany them. No other dictionary for native speakers attempts this on such a scale.

In British English, a full stop is also the only punctuation mark necessary in many longer sentences which contain more than one complete statement or idea, provided the parts of the sentence are closely connected to each other in sense or theme and are joined by a linking word or words such as *and*, *because* or *so that/in order*, as in the following examples:

She got up early and went out for a long walk.

I go to the supermarket on Saturdays because it is the only day of the week I have free.

She makes soup from the chicken bones so that nothing is wasted.

He did a second job in the evenings in order to earn some extra money for life's little luxuries.

➤ See also Chapter 17, where the conventions of American English punctuation are summarized.

Full stop or comma?

A common error in punctuation is to use a comma where a full stop is required. Consider the following examples:

✗ The caterpillars of the cabbage white butterfly will destroy your brassicas in a matter of days, rabbits will do the same.

✗ Colin will be twelve in September, Michael is more than two years younger.

In both examples there are two complete statements with no connecting word or words between them. As they stand, they must be written as two sentences separated by a full stop:

✓ The caterpillars of the cabbage white butterfly will destroy your brassicas in a matter of days. Rabbits will do the same.

✓ Colin will be twelve in September. Michael is more than two years younger.

Alternatively, if you want to show a connection or contrast between the two statements, you can do so by adding a connecting word such as *and* or *but* between the two statements. Then it is correct to separate the two statements with a comma, and only one full stop is required at the end of the connected statements.

✓ The caterpillars of the cabbage white butterfly will destroy your brassicas in a matter of days, and rabbits will do the same.

✓ Colin will be twelve in September, but Michael is more than two years younger.

(It is also correct to punctuate two-part sentences of this type with a semicolon. More of this in Chapter 7.)

Over-use of the full stop

Another common error is to separate into two sentences information that should belong in a single sentence. A full stop is inserted where no punctuation or only a comma is necessary, as in the following examples:

✗ There were no clues. As to what had happened.

✗ Many building societies converted to banks in the nineties. Of which the Halifax was the largest.

In the examples above, the second sentence cannot stand alone, and should be written as follows:

✓ There were no clues as to what had happened.

✓ Many building societies converted to banks in the nineties, of which the Halifax was the largest.

Use of the full stop in partial sentences

However, there are other sentence fragments (or partial sentences) which are very common in ordinary speech and can quite legitimately stand as separate sentences in certain kinds of writing.

Even though they don't contain a verb, partial sentences which are elliptical, or are inversions, or are very closely linked to the previous statement, can be written as separate sentences with full stops, as in:

✓ I don't hate her. Far from it.

✓ I do love you. Please believe me. I really honestly do.

✓ Will I make my fortune from writing? Very unlikely.

Remember that such elliptical sentences should not be used in formal written texts, such as business correspondence or reports. Their use should be confined to informal correspondence, journalism or creative writing. However, even in these contexts they should be used fairly sparingly unless you want to create a stilted or staccato effect for stylistic reasons.

Omission marks

The full stop mark or dot has another specialized use that affects the full stop normally used at the end of a sentence.

Omission marks or **suspension marks** (three dots printed one after the other and separated by thin spaces) are used to indicate that a sentence or statement has gradually tailed off into silence, or something further is implied but is not actually stated. (Omission marks are also used to indicate that the writer has quoted from another text but has not reproduced the quoted material in full. More on this in Chapter 8.)

Here we will deal with the effect that these marks have when they are used at the end of a sentence or statement.

Consider the following examples:

> Nothing she tried seemed to do any good. She was at her wits' end. The baby cried and cried…
>
> And so, dear reader, let us avert our eyes and leave these two young lovebirds to their billing and cooing …
>
> 'This gun's loaded. If you don't give me the money …'

The first example uses omission marks to show how the crying of the baby went on continously and relentlessly. In the second example, the writer is indicating to the reader that the couple's ongoing happiness is taken for granted and need not be described further. In the third example, the threat is left unfinished because what has been said already strongly implies that the person being threatened will be shot if they don't hand over the money.

From the point of view of punctuation, notice that in all these examples the sentence ends with only the three dots of the omission marks. Because their purpose is to indicate that the sentence is unfinished, it would be wrong to add a fourth dot: that is, a full stop. However, any new sentence after the three omission marks starts with a capital letter in the normal way.

The full stop in direct speech

When punctuating direct speech that comes at the end of a sentence and ends with a full stop, remember that the full stop comes inside the closing quotation mark. It is not necessary to add a second full stop outside the closing quotation mark:

✓ He said gently, 'I know you're unhappy.'

✗ He said gently, 'I know you're unhappy.'.

Note that when the quoted speech comes before the verbs of saying, wondering, etc, the full stop at the end of the quoted speech is replaced by a comma, as in:

'I know you're unhappy,' he said gently.

When the text in quotation marks comes at the end of a sentence, but what is inside the quotation marks is not direct speech, the full stop usually comes outside the closing quotation marks, as in:

At the bottom of each white cross were the words 'An unnamed soldier who fell in the Great War of 1914–18'.

Full stop, question mark or exclamation mark?

Uncertainty and error may also arise from the fact that it is sometimes not immediately obvious whether it is correct to use a full stop, or an exclamation mark, or a question mark. This problem is dealt with in more detail in the following two chapters, but in general the correct punctuation mark to use is the one that matches the underlying meaning. For example, a full stop is used for requests that have a statement-like intonation, as in:

Would all sixth-form students who want to take study leave please give their details as soon as possible to a staff member in the school office.

Could you pass me the salt and pepper, please.

Note that in the second example it would also be correct to use a question mark.

A full stop should also be used for indirect questions, as in:

✓ Ask her who said that.

✓ She asked if he would be able to attend a meeting the following Thursday.

➤ For information on how the full stop is used in abbreviations, see Chapter 13.

2

The question mark

A **question mark** (?) is also known as an **interrogation mark**.

It is one of two possible substitutes for a full stop at the end of a sentence. The other is the exclamation mark, which is discussed in the next chapter. Remember that a question mark at the end of a sentence may be the only indication to a reader that the sentence is a question rather than a statement, and thus should be read with the appropriate expression and tone. Compare the following examples:

> You've had your lunch.
>
> You've had your lunch?

The first example is a statement of fact and so is punctuated with a full stop. The second example is the kind of elliptical question commonly used in speech, and this is signalled by the question mark.

Direct questions

The question mark is used at the end of sentences that are direct questions, as in:

> What's that you've got there?
>
> Is it cold outside?
>
> Which language does the word 'moccasin' come from?
>
> Should I wait for you or go straight back home?
>
> What business is it of yours?
>
> Haven't you got a warmer coat? You look as if you're freezing to death.
>
> I don't know your older brother, do I?
>
> Do you realize who you're talking to?

If the direct question is a quotation in the actual words of the speaker, a question mark comes at the end of the question, inside the closing quotation mark or marks, as in:

> 'Do you realize who you're talking to?' she asked indignantly.
>
> Then he said, 'Who would like some brandy?'
>
> 'What does he intend to do with that big pile of bricks?' 'You may well ask!'

Indirect questions

Remember that a question mark should not be used at the end of a sentence that contains an indirect question. Instead, use a full stop, as in:

> I asked her what she was holding in her hand.
>
> Ask him what he intends to do with that big pile of bricks.

Note, in particular, the second example above. It is a command (which happens to contain an indirect question) and, as such, is punctuated with a full stop.

It is also easy to fall into the trap of using a question mark with an indirect question when the sentence is long and seems, at first sight, to be interrogative, as in the following example:

> ✗ But the really interesting question is what will take its place in this vital prime time slot?
>
> ✓ But the really interesting question is what will take its place in this vital prime time slot.

There are, however, a couple of instances when it is correct to punctuate an indirect question with a question mark. The first of these is when the indirect question is expressing a polite command, as in the first example below. The second is when the indirect question is, in reality, expressing a tentative direct request, as in the second example below.

> Will you please move back?
>
> I was wondering if you'd like to join us for dinner this evening?

Other uses of the question mark

Sometimes, and especially in rhetorical questions, more than one question mark is used as a way of signalling very strong feelings, such as indignation, as in:

> Who the hell does she think she is???

While this is quite acceptable for personal correspondence, it is widely considered to be bad style in most other contexts, and should be avoided, in particular, in formal writing and correspondence.

The question mark is also used inside parentheses to draw attention to something that is questionable or uncertain in a text or statement, as in:

> They signed the register as Mr and Mrs Smith (?) and asked for champagne to be sent up to their room.
>
> St Patrick [389–?493], patron saint of Ireland, was born in Britain, probably somewhere in Wales.

3

The exclamation mark

An **exclamation mark** (**!**) is also called (especially in American usage) an **exclamation point**.

It is one of two possible substitutes for a full stop at the end of a sentence. The other is the question mark, discussed in the previous chapter. As with the question mark, an exclamation mark may be the only indication to the reader of the way that the sentence should be read: that is, whether the writer's words should be read as a matter-of-fact statement, an exclamation, or a question. Compare the following examples, all of which are correctly punctuated:

> You've tidied your room.[= statement]
>
> You've tidied your room![= exclamation]
>
> You've tidied your room?[= question]

An exclamation mark is the usual punctuation in interjections such as *There, there!*, *Hell!*, *Whoops!* and *Tut, tut!* It can be used to indicate a tone of surprise (as is shown in the example in the last paragraph), or some other strong emotion such as admiration, anger, frustration or desperation. Here are some more examples:

> How you've grown!
>
> What a beautiful picture!
>
> Don't you dare swear at me, you little twerp!
>
> I don't believe it!
>
> Help! I'm falling! Aargh!

The exclamation mark used to show emphasis

The exclamation mark is also used in certain other expressions that are emphatic statements of the speaker's opinion, such as:

> Oh no, not that old chestnut again!
>
> What a fool I've been!

Exclamatory questions

Remember that an exclamation mark is the correct punctuation mark to use in what is known as exclamatory questions: that is, sentences that have the form of a question but are, in fact, exclamations. Here are some examples:

> What the blazes are you doing!
>
> Isn't this great!
>
> Wasn't that a marvellous surprise!

Imperatives

Notice also that certain expressions that are imperative in tone and intent may or may not end with an exclamation mark, depending on the degree of emphasis used by the speaker, as in:

> 'Sit down, all of you.'
>
> No one moved.
>
> 'Sit down when I tell you!' he shouted.

Position in quotations

If the exclamation is a quotation in the actual words of the speaker, the exclamation mark is placed at the end of the exclamation, inside the closing quotation mark or marks, as in:

> She screamed at the top of her voice, 'I hate you, you swine!'
>
> 'Don't you dare touch me!' he shrieked.

Where exclamation marks should be avoided

All the previous examples are used in any kind of writing that tries to represent speech, and where the exclamation mark is necessary to convey the appropriate tone. However, where an objective and more formal style of writing is expected, such as in reports and business correspondence, exclamation marks should generally be avoided.

In particular, in formal writing, do not use an exclamation mark as a means of emphasizing the point you are trying to make, as in:

> ✗ We recommend that you proceed with extreme caution!
>
> ✓ We recommend that you proceed with extreme caution.

This style is only acceptable in informal writing, such as when using the informal conversational style adopted in many personal letters, as in:

It was a real tonic to see you all last weekend!

Your kindness and hospitality was much appreciated!

In informal writing, an exclamation mark is sometimes used to show that what has just been said is a jokey comment or aside, as in:

He's quite amazing for someone of his age. He'll want to take up skydiving next!

Other uses of the exclamation mark

A series of exclamation marks, or a mixture of exclamation and question marks, is sometimes used at the end of a phrase or sentence to emphasize the strength of emotion being expressed, as in:

I was really furious!!!

Really?!

This is acceptable for personal letters, but should never be used elsewhere, and especially not in formal correspondence.

An exclamation mark within parentheses is sometimes used to draw attention to something in a statement or sentence that the writer finds surprising, or to indicate an interpolation, as in:

Although he said he quite enjoyed (!) being ill, he was clearly depressed that morning.

Their (frequent!) visits were becoming increasingly irksome.

Again, this style should be avoided in formal writing.

4

The apostrophe

The origin of **apostrophe** (') is the ancient Greek word *apostrophos* meaning 'accent or mark of elision' [= a mark denoting something has been passed over or omitted]. It still has this function today in shortened forms such as *I've* for *I have*, *can't* for *cannot*, *the '50s* for *the 1950s*, and *the '45 rebellion* for *the 1745* [Jacobite] *rebellion*. It also appears in the poetic *'twas* for *it was* and *e'er* for *ever*; and, in compound nouns that contain a shortened word, such as *will-o'-the-wisp* for *will of the wisp*, and *ne'er-do-well* for *never do well*.

The apostrophe is also sometimes used to indicate that a word is a clipped form of a longer one: *'bus* for *omnibus*, *'plane* for *aeroplane*, *'flu* for *influenza*, and *'cello* for *violoncello*. Nowadays the apostrophe is omitted in these clipped forms, and is generally only seen in older texts. However, there are certain clipped forms that continue to be written with an apostrophe. These include: *o'clock* for *of the clock*; and the informal *'cos* for *because*.

Note that where *and* is shortened to *'n'* there are two apostrophes, as in: *rock'n'roll*, *salt'n'vinegar crisps*.

Misuse of the apostrophe

As a general rule, **never** add an apostrophe in ordinary (that is, non-possessive) plurals, as in:

✗ AUBERGINE'S 50p

✗ CREAM TEA'S

✗ The boy's walked down the street.

The first two examples contain the so-called grocer's apostrophe, often seen in signs or price lists in shop windows and advertising boards displayed by various retail premises and other businesses. All these examples are wrong, not least because a reader could be forgiven for musing to him- or herself, 'How did an aubergine get

50p and is it investing it wisely?' or 'The boy's *what* walked down the street?'

Nor should an apostrophe be used in the possessive pronouns *hers*, *theirs*, *ours* and *yours* or the possessive determiner *its*. This is a very common error, and one which shows that the offender has not yet got to grips with a very basic rule of grammar.

Remember, in particular, that *it's* with an apostrophe is **not** the possessive form, but is rather the short form of *it is*. Notice that the apostrophe in the shortened form *it's* comes before, not after, the *s*.

✗ The bull was stamping it's feet and bellowing at the top of it's lungs.

✓ The bull was stamping its feet and bellowing at the top of its lungs.

✗ Its' nearly 10 o'clock.

✗ Its nearly 10 o'clock.

✓ It's nearly 10 o'clock.

Remember too that the possessive form of *who* is *whose*; *who's* with an apostrophe is the short form of *who is*. Compare the following examples:

✗ Who's coat is this?

✓ Whose coat is this?

✗ Whose that at the door?

✓ Who's that at the door?

Notice however, that an apostrophe is used in the possessive pronoun *one's*, as in:

✓ A trip in such a small aircraft is unlikely to cure one's fear of flying.

Exceptions to the rules

An apostrophe is allowed in some ordinary plurals, such as the plurals of certain short words, individual letters, numbers, and abbreviations made up of lower case letters. For these plurals, the chance that the reader may hesitate or mispronounce what is written is avoided by the addition of the apostrophe. Here are some examples:

It's one of those posh do's.

All the houses have lean-to's at the back.

Dot your i's and cross your t's.

Mind your p's and q's.

How many s's are there in Mississippi?

You can't have two ps's: only the first should be a ps; the second should be pps.

She got two A's and two B's in her A-levels.

He got two 1's, three 2's and three 3's in his Standard Grades.

Mummy, are these baby goats he's or she's?

There is another instance when it is permissible to add an apostrophe in a non-possessive plural, and that is when the plural is the title of a book or play, as in:

There have been two Macbeth's [= two different versions of the play *Macbeth*] staged in Glasgow this summer.

The apostrophe indicating possession

When an apostrophe is used to indicate possession it may be used with or without a following *s*. The basic rule for singular and plural nouns that end in *s* is: write what you hear and say. If an extra *s* is added in the pronunciation of the possessive form add *'s* in the written form. However, if it sounds too clumsy to add a second *s*, add an apostrophe only. The following is more detailed guidance on the use of apostrophes in possessive forms.

- For singular nouns and names that do not end with a letter *s*, the possessive case is formed by adding *'s*, as in the following examples:

  Holly's hair is getting darker as she gets older.

  The child's hands were cut and bleeding.

  This coat is Mary's, I think.

  Note that when possession applies to two or more named individuals, the *'s* is added to the last name only, as in:

  Do you have John and Adele's address?

  On Tom and Mrs Trollope's return to Paris in 1839, they were 'overwhelmed with invitations and social attentions of all kinds'.

- For plural nouns that do not end in letter *s*, the possessive case is also formed by adding *'s*, as in the following examples:

The children's education is more important than anything else.

the people's love of ceremony

the men's hostel

- **For singular or mass nouns and names that end in *s*, the possessive case is usually formed by adding *'s*, as in:**

  These are James's CDs

  a photograph of Angus's mother and father

  my boss's car

  the bus's rear bumper

  my brother Charles's boat

  the octopus's normal food

  get your money's worth

  in Jesus's name

  With singular nouns and names that end in the letter *s*, if in doubt, add *'s*.

  However, notice that an apostrophe without a following *s* is used in names ending in *-es* (which may effectively be treated like plurals); and, this is also the convention (though *'s* is also used) in certain others names, including names from the Bible and classical literature, eg:

  That is John Hodges' house.

  Ulysses' wife

  Moses' parting of the Red Sea

  Keats' poems

  Jesus' mother, Mary

  Herodotus' Histories

  Xerxes' army

- **For plural nouns and names that end in *s*, the possessive case is formed by adding an apostrophe only, as in:**

  the ladies' room

  the Joneses' garden

  the Wales' first child

  the Rolls' engine

  two dollars' worth [= the amount two dollars will buy]

  three months' holiday [= a holiday of three months]

They represent the bosses' side of industry.

The octopuses' tank needs cleaning.

A final point on the use of apostrophes. It is no longer necessary to have an apostrophe in the expression *for goodness sake*, even though, strictly speaking, the noun 'goodness' is in the possessive case [= for the sake of goodness]. Thus, *for goodness's sake* is now never used, and *for goodness' sake* is becoming rare.

5

The comma

The **comma** (,) is probably the most used, and the most abused, punctuation mark of all. Commas are used inside a sentence, between the capital letter at the beginning of the sentence and the full stop (or full-stop equivalents) at the end of the sentence.

The comma is often said to indicate a short pause or slight interruption in a sentence, and while this is broadly its function, the description is not particularly helpful as a guide to how sentences are or should be punctuated with commas. While it is obviously very important to know where a comma should be inserted, it is almost as important to know when not to use one.

Summary of the uses of the comma discussed in this chapter

- Commas marking off the items in a list of three or more items.
- Commas enclosing supplementary or subordinate information within a sentence.
- A comma separating two main clauses in a compound sentence.
- A comma marking the end of a subordinate clause when, by inversion, the subordinate clause precedes the main clause of a sentence.
- A comma separating the main clause of a sentence from a following subordinate clause that expresses a result or consequence.
- Commas grouping words together to clarify or change their meaning.
- Commas indicating an omission or ellipsis.
- A comma indicating a slight pause made in speech.

Commas in lists

Commas are used where lists of parallel items not linked by a conjunction occur within a sentence. These parallel items may be single words (nouns, adjectives or some other part of speech) or, they may be phrases.

Here are some straightforward examples with lists of nouns:

> She grows potatoes, carrots, beans and onions.
>
> Alice, Siobhan and Liam will be coming to the party too.

Notice that the commas are used to avoid repeating the conjunction 'and' after each item in the list, as in:

> She grows potatoes and carrots and beans and onions.
>
> Alice and Siobhan and Liam will be coming to the party too.

Commas in lists are therefore often used as substitutes for linking words or conjunctions.

When the last two items are already linked by a conjunction (as here and in many other such lists), it is not necessary to insert a comma before the conjunction. Remember that punctuation in British texts is kept to the minimum necessary to convey the meaning clearly and, according to this criterion, the comma before the conjunction + final item is not required. However, a comma in this position is not incorrect, and in American style it is preferred, as in:

> ✓ She grows potatoes, carrots, beans, and onions.
>
> ✓ Alice, Siobhan, and Liam will be coming to the party too.

Of course, in both British and American usage, commas are obligatory after all the other items in the list: that is, after 'potatoes' and 'carrots' in the first example, and after 'Alice' in the second example.

In more complex lists, it is often necessary to insert a comma before the conjunction + final item, to avoid ambiguity:

> The series will include material from some of Britain's most popular and innovative comedians – Tommy Cooper, Morecambe and Wise, Tony Hancock, and Reeves and Mortimer.

If there was no comma after 'Hancock' the reader may be misled into thinking that 'Tony Hancock and Reeves' belong together.

Here are some more examples of the comma used in lists:

Culture is an integrated system of beliefs, values and customs.

Many of them find work in shops, cafes, and transport services.

The wooden cooking utensils, hand-carved sticks and Loden capes in the Alpine shops are good value for money.

Leading goal-scorers in the 1998 World Cup were David Sukor of Croatia, Gabriel Batistuta of Argentina, Christian Vieri of Italy, Ronaldo of Brazil, Marcelo Salas of Chile, and Luis Hernandez of Mexico.

When the list is made up of multiple adjectives preceding a noun, commas are usually added in the same way as for nouns. Here are some examples:

It is a quiet, comfortable hotel close to the sea.

In his outstretched hand was an unremarkable, small and misshapen lump of what appeared to be dirty glass.

Where only two adjectives precede the noun, and these adjectives are not linked by 'and', the comma can sometimes be omitted. However, think carefully before omitting a listing comma, because its presence or absence can sometimes alter the implied meaning of what is written. Consider the following example:

A short, bearded butler showed them into the study.

With the comma, it is clear that the butler is short and also has a beard.

Now look at the same sentence with the comma omitted:

A short bearded butler showed them into the study.

Is the butler or his beard short? It isn't quite clear, so the comma is needed to clarify the meaning.

Now look at the next example:

The endangered white rhino is now being successfully bred in captivity.

Here, if a comma is inserted after 'endangered' the sentence would be over-punctuated. The reason is that the adjectives 'endangered' and 'white' do not modify the same thing. Grammatically-speaking, the second adjective modifies the noun 'rhino', but the first modifies both 'white' and 'rhino'. The adjectives should not be separated by a comma.

Here are some more examples of sentences with lists of adjectives that should not be separated by commas:

> Just inside the gate was a great big dog.
>
> She wore a pair of antique Spanish earrings made of solid gold.
>
> The Grand Old Duke of York, he had 10 000 men.

A useful test to help you decide whether or not there should be a comma between two adjectives is to substitute an 'and' for the comma. If the sense is clear with the 'and' instead of the comma, this indicates that a comma is needed between the adjectives.

Apply the test to the first two examples above. Neither 'a great and big dog' or 'antique and Spanish earrings' would be said or written, so it is correct to omit the commas.

Look again at the 'butler' example from earlier in the chapter: 'a short and bearded butler' is a feasible rephrasing, so a comma is necessary.

Enclosing extra information within a sentence

When a pair of commas encloses supplementary or subordinate information within a sentence they function in much the same way as a pair of brackets. The words within the commas are effectively isolated from the rest of the sentence by the commas, and do not interrupt the flow or sense of the sentence. In this way, they are rather like a verbal aside, which you hear but which doesn't divert you from the main topic of conversation.

Here are some examples of commas used in this way:

> He maintained that he, as the only surviving male, had a legitimate claim to the throne.
>
> It was her opinion, she told Rory, that there was something awfully funny going on.
>
> The semi-autobiographical *David Copperfield* was first published, as were all Dickens' novels, in serial form.
>
> A second earthquake, less severe than the first, caused minor damage.
>
> Mr Blair, the Prime Minister, cut short his holiday in France.
>
> Janey, like her mother before her, is a very competent horsewoman.

We have decided, after careful consideration, not to accept your offer.

She had, of course, no other choice.

Carol, who hated being the centre of attention, was extremely embarrassed and, not waiting to hear any more, fled.

Remember that in all these sentences a **pair of commas** must be used. One of the commonest punctuation errors is to forget to insert one of the commas, so that the supplementary information is no longer isolated from the rest of the sentence. This can alter the sense completely. Compare the following examples:

✓ Malcolm, who you already know, is related to me by marriage and is a regular houseguest.

✗ Malcolm, who you already know is related to me by marriage and is a regular houseguest.

Note that omission of the second comma changes the sense.

An effective test to check whether a pair of commas should be used (and also where they should be placed) is to omit the supplementary phrase altogether. If the sentence still makes sense without it, this shows that the phrase should be enclosed in a pair of commas.

Apply this test to the last example:

Malcolm is related to me by marriage and is a regular houseguest.

The sentence still makes sense, so 'who you already know' should be enclosed in a pair of commas.

Another common error is to position one or other of the commas wrongly. Again, the test outlined above will show whether or not you have got it right. Look at the following example:

He got to his feet, and clearing his throat loudly a couple of times, began to speak.

Now, remove the words within the commas, and see what you are left with:

✗ He got to his feet began to speak.

There is obviously something wrong here. One of the commas must be in the wrong place. Look again and you will quickly see that the first comma should come after the 'and'. Move the comma, and now remove the words within the commas:

✓ He got to his feet and began to speak.

Success!

The situation is further complicated when a sentence contains a relative clause. A relative clause is one that usually (but not always) begins with a relative pronoun such as 'who', 'which' or 'that'. The relative clauses in the following examples are underlined:

Carol, *who hated being the centre of attention*, was extremely embarrassed.

The thing *that annoys me most* is that he doesn't seem to care.

The villagers, *who make their living by crofting*, have protested at the reduction in the levels of subsidy.

And, an example without a relative pronoun:

The book *I'm looking for* isn't in its usual place.

When punctuation is being considered, it is important to know the difference between a relative clause that makes a comment or gives additional information about the noun it refers to, and one which serves to identify or pick out the noun it refers to. The first type (**non-defining relative clauses**) are separated off from the rest of the sentence by being enclosed in a pair of commas. However, the second type (**defining relative clauses**) are not.

Consider one of the previous examples again:

The villagers, who make their living by crofting, have protested at the reduction in the levels of subsidy.

Here, 'who make their living by crofting' is a non-defining relative clause. In other words, all, and not just some, of the villagers make their living by crofting.

But let's remove the commas:

The villagers who make their living by crofting have protested at the reduction in the levels of subsidy.

Now, 'who make their living by crofting' is a defining relative clause, and its effect is to restrict the application of the word 'villagers' to only some of the people who live in the village: that is, only those villagers who make their living by crofting.

Do you mean all the villagers or just some of them? Take care to punctuate the sentence according to the sense you want to convey.

Separating two main clauses

Look at this example, which has two main clauses:

John giggled, but Henry turned deathly pale.

The clauses have equal weight in this sentence, one clause contrasts with the other, and both clauses could, if necessary, stand alone as complete sentences.

In sentences where two main clauses are linked, the first clause must be followed by a comma.

Here are some more examples:

Gary was a very promising artist, yet he couldn't get a place in art college.

Great minds think alike, and fools seldom differ.

The Yukon is ideal for those of you who enjoy roughing it in the wilderness, but British Columbia is a less challenging holiday destination for the average tourist.

Marking a subordinate clause that precedes a main clause

When a subordinate clause beginning with words like 'when', 'how', 'since', and 'although' is placed at the beginning of a sentence before the main clause, a comma must be inserted after the last word in the subordinate clause.

Here are some examples that illustrate this use of the comma:

When he arrived home, the children ran to hug him.

As soon as she heard the news, she booked a seat on the first flight home.

Because he was blind, he had to be helped across the road.

Since the majority has voted in favour, planning permission for the proposed development is hereby granted.

Soon after her daughter was born, she developed post-natal depression.

Although he was still weak, he managed to have a little walk around the garden.

Separating a main clause from a 'result' clause

When a subordinate clause expresses a result or consequence of the action referred to in the main clause, the subordinate clause should usually be separated from the main clause by a comma, as in:

She works night shifts, so her mother looks after the children during the day.

All the lights went out, so we had to eat by candlelight.

But, when the subordinate clause is linked to the main clause by the conjunction 'and', no comma is necessary:

Write on the walls of your bedroom again and there'll be no TV for a month.

Grouping words to clarify or change their meaning

Sometimes it is necessary to clarify the structure or meaning of a written sentence by inserting a visual break. The comma serves this purpose and avoids the danger of the reader being misled by the juxtaposition of words that do not actually belong together.

Look at these sentences and notice how the presence or absence of a comma, or its position, changes the sense:

He was sick, and tired of trying to make a living in a place that was so obviously dying on its feet.

He was sick and tired of trying to make a living in a place that was so obviously dying on its feet.

For one week only, coats will be half-price.

For one week, only coats will be half-price.

Outside the square was a seething mass of angry demonstrators.

Outside, the square was a seething mass of angry demonstrators.

Take care, however, not to insert a clarifying comma that has the effect of separating the subject from the verb, as in:

✗ The dress that she wore to the party, is the one she bought in Paris.

✓ The dress that she wore to the party is the one she bought in Paris.

But, when two identical words are juxtaposed, a comma may be inserted between them to avoid confusion:

✓ What sort of husband he is, is of no interest to his employer.

✓ If she can, can you let me know.

Indicating an omission or ellipsis

A comma may be used to show that one or more words already used earlier in the sentence have been omitted, as in:

Some groups will be travelling by train; others, by coach.

Indicating a slight pause made in speech

A comma or commas should be inserted to mark off a sentence adverb; a commenting word inserted into a sentence; a vocative noun or noun phrase; and words such as 'yes', 'no' or 'please' when they are part of a longer sentence.

Here are some examples:

Nevertheless, she can't be expected to do it all immediately.

However, this isn't what we're here to talk about today.

Soon after Michaelmas, however, Bruce descended with his own considerable force into England.

You, Jim, are the person Harry has to liaise with over this.

Now, ladies and gentlemen, would you start moving through to the dining room, please.

Mary, do you know where my hairbrush is?

Two ice-cream cones, please.

No, I think you're wrong about that.

You'll have to retype the whole thing, I'm afraid.

When a comma should not be used

- Do not use a comma to link what are, in fact, two separate sentences.

  ✗ The caterpillars of the cabbage white butterfly will destroy your brassicas in a matter of days, rabbits will do the same.

  ✓ The caterpillars of the cabbage white butterfly will destroy your brassicas in a matter of days. Rabbits will do the same.

- Do not use a comma when the two parts of a sentence are closely connected to each other in sense or theme and are joined by a linking word such as 'and', 'because' or 'that'.

  ✗ He was tired, because he had stayed up until 3 a.m.

  ✓ He was tired because he had stayed up until 3 a.m.

  ✗ Penny told you yesterday, that she might be a little late for work this morning.

  ✓ Penny told you yesterday that she might be a little late for work this morning.

- **Do not mistakenly insert a comma after adverbs or adverbial phrases unless this is the sense you intend.**

  The British research and development establishments were, curiously, reluctant to employ them.

  The British research and development establishments were curiously reluctant to employ them.

  Of course, she was lying.

  Of course she was lying.

  Both pairs of examples are punctuated correctly. However, in the first pair the use of commas changes the function of the adverb: 'curiously' applies to the whole sentence in the first sentence, and only to 'reluctant' in the second. In the second pair, the omission of the comma changes the 'of course' from a comment to a confirmation. Take care to punctuate the sentence according to how you want it to be read.

Commas in letter-writing

Formerly, in both handwritten and typewritten letters, it was usual to follow each line of the address with a comma. A comma was also inserted after the building number, as in:

Mr R. Galbraith,
5a, Henderson Avenue,
ABERDEEN
AB3 6FG.

Nowadays, in line with the general tendency in British English to use the minimum of punctuation, these commas are usually omitted, particularly in typewritten letters or those produced on a word processor:

Mr R Galbraith
5a Henderson Avenue
ABERDEEN
AB3 6FG.

If the date on the letter is written in the order day + month + year, no comma is required between the month and the year, as in:

30th August 1998

30 August 1998

However, if the order is month + day + year, a comma must be inserted between the day and the year, as in:

August 30, 1998

Similarly, if the day is named, a comma should be inserted between the name and number of the day, as in:

Sunday, 30 August 1998

➤ For the use of commas with direct speech see Chapter 8 Quotation Marks.

6

The colon

The principal use of the **colon** (:) in ordinary texts is to indicate that what follows explains, expands on, or completes the part that has gone before. What follows the colon may be a complete sentence, a list, or even a single word. Here are some examples of sentences punctuated by colons:

I've got some really exciting news: Kirsty got the job in London.

It is certainly the best book I have read on the subject: well-researched, amusing, and packed with fascinating information.

He has one of those pompous-sounding titles: Executive in Charge of Stationery Fastenings, or something of that kind.

Delays may be experienced when week-day traffic is heaviest: that is, between 7 a.m. and 9.30 a.m. and 4.30 p.m. and 7 p.m.

We made mountains of sandwiches: cheese and pickle, ham, roast beef, and lettuce and tomato.

The man was lying face down in the gutter: dead.

The following pupils have been awarded certificates of merit: Andrew Hetherington, Sheila Monaghan, Brian Wilkie, Mark Willis, and Robert Douglas.

All the time she was at the health farm she thought of one thing, and one thing only: food.

Sometimes, the explanation or expansion may precede the main or more general part of the sentence, as in:

'Bringing Up Baby', 'The Man Who Came to Dinner', 'Gone with the Wind': all films I would happily watch again and again.

What follows the colon may be a longer list with each item on a new line.

For wallpapering, you should have the following equipment:
a pasting table
a pasting brush
a paper-hanging brush
a broom
a clean bucket with a handle
a wallpaper trough
wallpaper scissors

Where each item in the list appears on a new line a dash is sometimes placed immediately after the colon. This is unnecessary but not wrong. However, when the items in the list follow the colon on the same line, a dash should never be used between the colon and the first item of the list:

✗ He grows all sorts of vegetables:- peas, beans, carrots, onions and cauliflower.

It is not correct to insert a colon after the verb *to be*.

✗ In these situations, by far the most important thing is: keep calm.

The sentence should be reworded.

✓ In these situations, by far the most important thing is to keep calm.

A colon may also be used in sentences made up of two parts, where one part balances or contrasts with the other (rather than expanding, explaining or completing it), as in:

To err is human: to forgive, divine.

Sulky scowls and sneers from the two sisters: blushes and giggles from their friends.

But note that, nowadays, a semicolon is almost invariably preferred in this position.

To err is human; to forgive, divine.

Sulky scowls and sneers from the two sisters; blushes and giggles from their friends.

Direct speech and quotations

A colon may be used, in strictly limited ways, to introduce direct speech or quoted material from another piece of writing.

It is acceptable to use a colon before an opening quotation mark when the quoted speech has the effect of elaborating or expanding what has gone before the colon, as in:

What Trollope wrote in *Phineas Redux* is as true now as it was then: 'What man thinks of changing himself so as to suit his wife? And yet men expect that women shall put on altogether new characters when they are married, and girls think that they can do so.'

Do not use a colon as a substitute for the conventional comma to introduce direct speech.

✗ He said: 'What do you mean by that?'

✓ He said, 'What do you mean by that?'

If you are using a long quotation, it can be separated off from the surrounding text by a colon at the end of the last line of main text, with a line space before and after the quotation.

This is clearly illustrated by Daniel's assertion that:

> All the facts with which a grammar deals are to be found in the language to which the grammar belongs; and it is in the language itself, not in books, that these facts are to be primarily sought. Grammarians do not impose rules on the language; they merely collect from the language rules already in existence, and set them forth in an orderly way.

Some more uses of the colon

Colons are used between numbers to indicate ratios.

49:28 = 7:4

For formal writing, it is preferable to write out ratios in full.

The devastating range of the longbow and the skill of the archers won the battle for the English, though they were outnumbered by the French by nearly three to one.

Colons are used after headings in certain types of business correspondence, such as memos.

To: ...

cc: ...

From: ...

Date: ...

But, you should not use a colon after a heading that starts a new section in other non-business texts.

✗ Some more uses of the colon:

A colon is also used in the titles of books or other publications where there is a main title followed by a subtitle or subsidiary title.

Depopulation in the Scottish Highlands: a statistical survey

7

The semicolon

The **semicolon** (;) has two distinct functions. The first of these is to mark a stronger and more definite break in a sentence than a comma, but less of a break than that between two separate sentences, where a full stop is used. The second use of the semicolon is in long lists, where several items in the list can be logically grouped together and separated from other items or groups of items within the list.

The semicolon between clauses in a sentence

A semicolon may be used to join two clauses to make a longer more complex sentence, with the semicolon taking the place of a comma followed by a conjunction such as 'and' or 'but'.

Remember that a semicolon is only used where the two clauses may otherwise stand as two complete sentences: whenever a semicolon is used, there is also, in principle, the option of using a full stop instead. The use of a semicolon makes the relationship between the two clauses closer than two separate sentences would, but creates a stronger break than a linking comma + a conjunction. It has the effect of balancing or contrasting what is said in one clause and what is said in the following clause.

Here are some examples of sentences where semicolons mark the break between clauses:

A crocodile is a reptile; a whale is a mammal.

There's no more to be said; the matter is closed.

Children at play are not playing about; their games should be seen as their most serious-minded activity.

Traditionally many legal documents have been written without punctuation; in modern documents punctuation is more common.

From Germany there is *The End of the History of Art*; from Britain comes a group of essays entitled *The New Art History*; from the United States has recently come *Rethinking Art History*; from Canada there is a forthright title *Art History: its use and abuse*.

In all these examples the clauses separated by the semicolon could stand as separate sentences. In all but the last example, the semicolon could be replaced by a connecting word or conjunction.

Do not use a semicolon when the second part of the sentence is not a complete clause.

Look at the following examples:

✗ I wasn't bothered; not in the least.

✗ The news that sent shockwaves around the world; the assassination of President Kennedy.

In each case, the last part of the sentence is a phrase, not a clause, and therefore neither example can be punctuated by a semicolon. The first should have a comma and the second a colon:

✓ I wasn't bothered, not in the least.

✓ The news that sent shockwaves around the world: the assassination of President Kennedy.

In general, when the clauses are connected by a conjunction, the punctuation mark to use between the clauses is a comma rather than a semicolon. But, certain connecting words are preceded by a semicolon. These include *however*, *hence*, *thus*, *therefore*, *meanwhile*, *also*, *consequently*, and *nevertheless*.

Here are some examples of sentences that have one of these connecting words preceded by a semicolon:

She was standing right in front of him; however, he couldn't see her.

There were frantic attempts to save personal belongings; meanwhile, the water level continued to rise.

The goods were not delivered on the date specified; therefore, we have cancelled the order.

The semicolon in lists

In Chapter 5, the use of the comma in lists was discussed and exemplified. In general, the comma is the correct punctuation mark to use in lists. However, where a long list occurs in a sentence and some items (whether single words or phrases) within the list can be regarded as being part of a distinct group, a semicolon may be used to separate that group from the rest of the list and so make a stronger break than is made by a comma. This allows the reader to pause at a logical point in the sentence.

The following example illustrates this use of the semicolon:

> They publish English dictionaries, both for native speakers and learners of English; reference books and encyclopedias; and books of Scottish interest.

8

Quotation marks

Quotation marks – also known as **quotes** or **inverted commas** – are used principally, as their name suggests, to mark off quotations: that is, to enclose direct speech or exact quotations from written texts. Their other functions are to highlight certain words and phrases in a sentence, and to enclose titles.

Quotation marks are always used in pairs. There are two types: **single quotes** (**'**...**'**) and **double quotes** (**"**...**"**). Either single or double quotes may be used, but British style tends to favour single quotes. However, in some circumstances the use of double quotes is recommended, as will be explained later.

American style is to use double quotes. The differences between British and American usage are described in more detail in Chapter 17.

Here we concentrate on the conventions of British style, where single quotes are used when there is only one quotation. The situation becomes a little more complicated when there is a second quotation embedded within the first one. In such cases, the first quotation is marked off by single quotes, and the embedded quotation is marked off by double quotes, as in:

> The assistant manager declared, 'These are "circumstances beyond my individual control", as Mr Micawber said.'

The first set of quotation marks mark off all the words actually spoken by the assistant manager. However, he has used not only his own words, but those of Mr Micawber, a character in Dickens' *David Copperfield*. The quotation within the quoted speech is therefore marked off by double quotes.

Enclosing a direct quotation

As is seen in the example above, quotation marks are used to mark off direct speech and direct quotations: that is, the exact words someone has spoken or written. Here are some more examples:

'Why can't I go?' asked Charlotte.

They chanted in unison, 'We want Owens!'

'To the true cynic', said Oscar Wilde, 'nothing is ever revealed.'

In direct speech, it is very important to remember that the quotation marks enclose only **the exact words** used by the speaker, and not a reported version of these words. Notice also, in the last example above, two sets of quotation marks are needed, because the quotation has been split into two parts.

It is a very common error to put quotes around indirect or reported speech. Compare the following examples:

✓ He nudged her and whispered, 'Do you want to leave now?' [= direct speech]

✓ He nudged her and asked in a whisper if she wanted to leave now. [= indirect speech]

✗ He nudged her and asked in a whisper 'if she wanted to leave now'. [= indirect speech]

Similarly, if a quotation is reworded so that it does not reproduce the original exactly, the quotation marks should then be moved to enclose the exact words, or should be dropped altogether.

The following examples reproduce Oscar Wilde's exact words:

Oscar Wilde said, 'To the true cynic nothing is ever revealed.'

As Oscar Wilde has it, 'To the true cynic nothing is ever revealed.'

Both are direct quotations and are therefore correctly enclosed by quotation marks.

However, if his words are expressed indirectly or their order is changed, they cannot then be enclosed in quotation marks:

✓ Oscar Wilde said that nothing is ever revealed to the true cynic.

✗ Oscar Wilde said that 'nothing is ever revealed to the true cynic'.

✓ Oscar Wilde said that 'nothing is ever revealed' to the true cynic.

A quotation that is no more than one sentence long should be incorporated into the surrounding sentence, within quotation marks, as in:

Shakespeare once said 'all the world's a stage'.

As Doctor Johnson put it in his famous *Dictionary of the English Language*, 'Every other author may aspire to praise; the lexicographer can only hope to escape reproach.'

Notice that in the first example (where the quotation is a short phrase) the full stop comes outside the closing quotation mark. In the second example, the quotation is a full sentence and the full stop comes inside the closing quotation mark.

Presentation of longer quotations

When a longer passage made up of four or more lines is being quoted, it can be treated as a new paragraph, but indented slightly from the left-hand margin. The introductory line is punctuated with a colon, and a one line space precedes and follows the quoted passage. Where this is done, it is not necessary to enclose the quoted passage with quotation marks.

This is clearly illustrated by Daniel's assertion that:

> All the facts with which a grammar deals are to be found in the language to which the grammar belongs; and it is in the language itself, not in books, that these facts are to be primarily sought. Grammarians do not impose rules on the language; they merely collect from the language rules already in existence, and set them forth in an orderly way.

How quotation marks affect other punctuation

The punctuation associated with quotation marks is a potential minefield.

As a general rule, punctuation marks that belong to, or are part of, the quoted speech or writing should be kept within the quotation marks; and, punctuation that belongs to the surrounding sentence goes outside the quotation marks. Usually a sentence that contains a quotation is punctuated like any other sentence and therefore the only additional punctuation required is the quotation marks themselves.

Example 1

'My parents are quite willing', she said, 'to look after the baby for the evening.'

Here a pair of bracketing commas has been added to mark off the interruption in the quotation. The commas are not part of the quoted speech, and have therefore been placed outside the quotation marks.

When bracketing commas are used in this way, many people prefer to place the first comma inside the first set of quotes, thus:

> 'My parents are quite willing,' she said, 'to look after the baby for the evening.'

This may seem illogical, since the comma is not part of the quotation. The advocates of this style say that it improves the appearance of the text, in that the comma comes immediately after the last letter. Using the first method, the comma 'floats' in white space.

It is really a matter of personal preference which you use, as long as you are consistent throughout any piece of writing. Some writers omit these bracketing commas altogether, but this is not recommended for essay writing or other texts where punctuation may be assessed or marked by someone with a more traditional view of correct punctuation.

Example 2

> 'You then, Andrew,' the teacher said, 'will be the captain of the yellow group.'

The first two commas belong to the quoted speech, and thus the second must come within the first closing quote. Neither the first nor the second comma may be omitted, but, as has been explained above, the third may:

> 'You then, Andrew,' the teacher said 'will be the captain of the yellow group.'

Example 3

> Jonathan kept repeating, 'Can I come in yet?'

Here, the question mark belongs to the quotation and thus should come inside the closing quotation mark. Notice that because the question mark is a full-stop equivalent, a full stop is not necessary after the closing quotation mark.

➤ Full stops with quotation marks are also discussed in Chapter 1.

Example 4

Did I hear him say, 'You can come in now'?

Notice that the question mark here belongs to the words *Did I hear him say* and not to the quoted speech, so it must come after the closing quotation mark. Again, because the end of the quotation and the end of the sentence coincide, only one full stop or full-stop equivalent is required (in this case, a question mark).

Example 5

Did I hear him say, 'What's for dinner?'?

Did I hear him say, 'What's for dinner?'

Did I hear him say, 'What's for dinner'?

In the first example there are two question marks, one inside the closing quote, and another outside it. This is the logical way to punctuate this sentence because *Did I hear him say* and *What's for dinner* are both questions, and so both require question marks. Many people regard this as rather excessive and prefer to use only one question mark, as in the other two examples. This diverges from the principle that quotations should be punctuated like any other sentence, but has a less fussy appearance.

Other uses of quotation marks

Single quotation marks (but never double quotation marks) are sometimes used by writers to highlight or set apart a word or phrase within a sentence. Quotes are used when words themselves are being discussed in writing: a technique that has, incidentally, been used for citing words throughout this book.

However, quotes are also used to mark off words that the writer wants to distance him- or herself from for a variety of reasons. Quotation marks used in this way are sometimes referred to as scare quotes. The word or phrase is not an actual quotation, but it may be jargon or slang, a cliché, a dialect word, a euphemistic term, or an archaic usage. The quotes are therefore a signal to the reader that the writer is not using his or her own voice for what is inside the quotes, or that he or she is being facetious, ironic or sarcastic. (In speech, it is these words that are sometimes accompanied by a gesture in which both index fingers are crooked to indicate inverted commas.)

Here are some examples:

> All the 'wee lassies' were about fifty and obviously not strangers to the biscuit tin.
>
> Apparently, the object of these sessions was to encourage us 'to get in touch with our feelings'.
>
> Aren't you being 'economical with the truth' when you say you know nothing about this?

Traditionally, the titles of books, plays, articles and poems were enclosed in quotations marks. This is still sometimes the case in handwritten texts, but elsewhere it is now more common to italicize titles. In academic writing, however, the titles of articles in journals and magazines, unpublished essays and dissertations, and the titles of chapters or sections of books are enclosed in quotes. The titles of books, plays, poems, films, newspapers, periodicals and classical works are italicized.

Problems with single quotation marks

The British preference for single rather than double quotation marks can cause difficulties in two sets of circumstances.

The first of these is when there is an apostrophe inside the quotation. Look at the following example:

> As Lilian Hellman said, 'I cannot and will not cut my conscience to suit this year's fashions.'

This doesn't create too much of a problem. But, look at the next example:

> She opined, 'Dickens' female characters were either hags or angels, and, as was so often the case, women were the victims of male writers' prejudices, caricatured or idealized.'

The reader could be forgiven for being at something of a loss to know where the quote ends. If double quotes were used here, no such confusion would arise.

> She opined, "Dickens' female characters were either hags or angels, and, as was so often the case, women were the victims of male writers' prejudices, caricatured or idealized."

The second problem relates to the highlighting function of quotation marks, where only single (never double) quotes are used. Again, if a highlighted word appears within a quotation marked off by single quotation marks, the reader might not know where the quote begins or ends.

> "Of course we all know how the meanings of words like 'gay' and 'wicked' have changed," she said.

9

Brackets

There are four different kinds of brackets: round brackets, square brackets, brace brackets and angle brackets.

Round brackets

For the purposes of this book, we will focus mainly on the commonest kind of brackets used in written or printed texts. These are **round brackets ( )**, also known as **parentheses**.

The broad function of round brackets is to enclose supplementary, but subordinate, information within a sentence or longer piece of text, isolating that information more effectively than would a pair of commas. Like bracketing commas, round brackets are a useful way of adding information without interfering too much with the reader's concentration on the sense of what appears before and after the brackets. A pair of dashes may be substituted for round brackets when the supplementary information represents a relatively strong interruption in the sentence.

More specifically, round brackets are used in the following ways:

- to include a clarification or explanation of what has gone before, as in the following examples:

  The majority of British families (57% at the last census) own their own homes.

  The model pictured left (gas or oil-fired) is available in six colours.

  We calculate that the labour input (total number of man-hours) for this contract will be 1400 hours.

  In the European Union, the concept of subsidiarity (the right of an individual member state's parliament to take decisions on issues that affect that member state) has been the subject of protracted debate.

- **to give additional or incidental information, as in:**

  With his father and sister, Mozart began a long tour (1764–65), during which they visited Germany, Belgium, Paris and London.

- **to enclose a comment by the writer, as in:**

  Camping (not everyone's cup of tea) is a relatively inexpensive option.

  My (admittedly rather amateurish) effort was rejected out of hand.

- **to include an example or examples, as in:**

  Many types of shellfish (for example, mussels and oysters) can be farmed quite readily given the correct conditions.

  Where the warm water of the Gulf Stream meets colder water from the Arctic (as here in the north-eastern states) fog is a common occurrence.

- **to identify or specify, as in:**

  Economists predict that the G7 countries (United States, Canada, Japan, Britain, France, Germany, and Italy) will have growth rates averaging 2.5% per annum.

  In their winter plumage, the redshank (*Tringa totanus*) and the spotted redshank (*Tringa erythropus*) are virtually indistinguishable at a distance.

- **to enclose an abbreviation following the full form, where the abbreviated form will be used again later in the text, as in:**

  Bovine spongiform encephalopathy (BSE) should therefore be eradicated from British herds by this date. There have been no reported cases of BSE in grass-fed herds.

- **to show equivalents or translations, as in:**

  Temperatures will fall to 15°C (59°F) in the late evening.

  Uisgebeatha (whisky) flowed freely and tartan-clad revellers whirled around the dance floor.

- **to enclose a reference to another part of the text or to other texts, as in:**

  For an expanded view, see page 24 (Fig. 3).

  The word *corf*, defined as 'a coalminer's basket, now usually a trolley or wagon', is from the Latin word *corbis*, a basket (Chambers Dictionary, 1998 edition).

- **as a space-saving method of indicating options, as in:**

  Any objection(s) should be made in writing to the Planning Department.

- **to enclose numbers or letters that highlight points within a sentence, as in:**

  Their declared aims and objectives were: (a) to bring the company back to profitablity within two years, and (b) to exploit new overseas markets.

  Where the number or letter is used to mark off a section or paragraph, the opening bracket is usually omitted, as in:

  1) Co-operative ventures.

  2) New product lines.

  3) Resources and staffing.

When brackets should not be used

Brackets should not be used to needlessly insert one independent clause, or sentence, within another.

✗ UN troops (all units are commanded by an officer experienced in peacekeeping duties) have been deployed along the cease-fire line.

Instead, a long sentence comment should follow the sentence it is commenting on and should start with a capital letter and end with a full stop, as in:

✓ UN troops have been deployed along the cease-fire line. All units are commanded by an officer experienced in peacekeeping duties.

Alternatively, the comment should be reworded to integrate more fully into the surrounding sentence, as in:

✓ UN troops (all units of which are commanded by an officer experienced in peacekeeping duties) have been deployed along the cease-fire line.

Important points relating to the use of brackets

Remember that brackets come in pairs, except where a closing bracket encloses a number in a list.

It is quite a common error for writers to forget to insert the closing bracket, especially when the bracketed information extends over more than one line.

An opening bracket should never stand on its own at the end of a line, nor should a closing bracket appear at the beginning of a line. There must be at least one word following an opening bracket before the text goes over to the next line, and at least one word preceding a closing bracket at the start of a new line.

Punctuation that belongs to the information that appears within the brackets should always be included within the brackets and not outside them.

A full sentence within brackets that is inserted into another sentence starts with a small letter and does not require a full stop, though it may take a question mark or an exclamation mark, as in:

> Old Grumpy (do you know who I mean?) has been making all our lives miserable.

Sometimes, it is necessary to have one pair of round brackets inside another pair, as in:

> The father of Alexander the Great (Philip II (382–336 BC) king of Macedon) organized the Greek states in a federal league, with himself as their general.

This practice should, for the sake of clarity, be kept to a minimum. Moreover, an opening or closing round bracket should not immediately follow another opening or closing round bracket, unless the particular structure of the text makes this completely unavoidable:

> ✗ The father of Alexander the Great (Philip II, king of Macedon (382–336 BC)) organized the Greek states in a federal league, with himself as their general.

Square brackets

Square brackets [ ] are used to enclose comments, corrections, explanations and queries introduced into a section of text by an editor or the writer, who has cited the passage concerned.

They also enclose the Latin word *sic* meaning 'thus', used to indicate that the quoted or cited passage contains an error or unconventional construction which the writer has not attempted to correct.

Braces

Braces { } are used singly or in pairs. A single brace is used to bring together several items on one side of the brace and link them with a single item on the other. They are used in pairs, for example in tables, to indicate alternatives, or to enclose an item that applies equally to items on either side of the pair of braces.

Angle brackets

The use of **angle brackets < >** is fairly technical, and need not concern us in this book. In summary, they are used to enclose words and figures, and to separate them from their context: for example, when a writer has supplied what is his or her likeliest guess or nearest approximation to an unknown, illegible or missing word, phrase, etc.

10

Dashes and slashes

The dash

The dash is a punctuation mark which, depending on its function and the text in which it appears, is printed in one of two lengths. The shorter of the two (–) is known as an **en dash** or **en rule**. The longer (—) is known as the **em dash** or **em rule**. ('Em' and 'en' are terms used in printing for measuring type, an en being half an em.) Both these lengths of dash may be used to separate off parts of a sentence (functioning in the same way as a pair of bracketing commas) but in this role the en dash is always preceded and followed by a white space, whereas the em dash is printed with no spaces before and after. Morever, the em dash is used less commonly nowadays for separating off parts of a sentence.

The dash, whether it is an en or an em dash, should be distinguished from the hyphen, which has a linking function and never appears with white space between it and the preceding or following letter. The hyphen is dealt with in the next chapter.

In handwritten texts, the dash used to mark off parts of a sentence is written as a single short line, surrounded by white space on either side. In typed texts, the dash (when it is marking off part of a sentence) is often represented by two hyphens (--). A double hyphen is used because there is not a longer line available on a typewriter keyboard. The same technique is sometimes used in word-processed texts to key a dash, but here the program usually recognizes that a dash is required and will automatically convert the double hyphen into an en dash.

Where a dash is used

In the following examples, note that where an em dash is used, it is closed up with the word that comes before and after. Alternatively, if an en dash is used, there is a space before and after the dash. The dash is used in the following ways:

- to enclose a parenthetical explanation, comment or aside. Notice that if the comment or explanation comes in the middle of the sentence, a **pair of dashes** must be used; if it comes at the end of the sentence, it is preceded by a single dash. Here are some examples:

  The appearance of the wood – the colour, the texture and the grain pattern – is the most important consideration when choosing the material for any woodworking project.

  Western influence is apparent as you walk the streets of the capital – Levi's, hamburger joints and *Dallas* on TV.

  He told me once—believe it if you will—that he had climbed every mountain in the French Alps.

  He had climbed every mountain in the French Alps – or so he told me once.

  But to my mind—though I am native here, and to the manner born—it is a custom more honour'd in the breach than in the observance.

  This curious whimsy might well have appealed to Henry Winstanley, the eccentric builder of the first—and most eccentric—Eddystone lighthouse.

  The dashes in these examples are used like a pair of bracketing commas. However, note that a pair of dashes usually signals a stronger or more emphatic interruption than do commas.

- to sum up what has gone before. In two-part sentences consisting of a general or summing-up statement followed by an itemized or more detailed explanation, the normal punctuation used is a colon, as in:

  There are some serious drawbacks in this particular scheme: its expense, its duration and its severe effects on the environment.

  However, if the sentence order is inverted, a dash may be used in place of the colon, as in:

  Its expense, its duration and its severe effects on the environment – these are some of the serious drawbacks of this particular scheme.

- to indicate that what follows the dash, or is enclosed by the dashes, has a more emphatic tone than what has gone before, as in:

She forgave him – or did she?

Unfortunately, there was nothing – absolutely nothing – that we could have done about it.

- to indicate that a sentence breaks off in the middle, as in:

  What really galls me is that he actually believed – oh, but what's the use of going on about it now?

  'Well, I'll be – ,' he muttered.

  This use of the dash is only appropriate to the kinds of writing in which actual conversation is being represented. It should not be used in formal writing.

- to avoid spelling out a swearword or expletive that may cause offence to readers. Nowadays, this is only used for the most extreme and taboo swearwords and expletives. But, it is interesting to note that the technique of using an em dash to replace parts of such words led to the formation of new milder forms of the original words: for example, 'Damn it!' was often written 'D— it!', hence 'Dash it!'; and, more recently, 'F— off!' has produced 'Eff off!'

The em dash is also sometimes used after a colon in lists where the items in the list each appear on a new line. But, when the items in the list follow immediately after the colon on the same line, do not insert a dash between the colon and the first word in the list. For examples see Chapter 6.

Some other uses of the en dash

In certain printed texts, the short dash (the en dash) is used with no surrounding white space in the following ways:

- to indicate ranges, as in:

  1914–1918

  103–105 Oxford Street

  pages 325–387

  Ranges are also indicated by the structures 'between X and Y' and 'from X to Y'. Notice that when a short dash is used, it replaces *both* 'between' and 'and' in the first structure, and *both* 'from' and 'to' in the second structure. It is bad style to use the structures 'between X–Y' and 'from X–Y', as in:

✗ There were between 25–35 vehicles involved in the collision.

✗ She lived there from 1967–68.

Instead, write:

✓ There were between 25 and 35 vehicles involved in the collision.

✓ There were 25–35 vehicles involved in the collision.

✓ She lived there from 1967 to 1968.

- **instead of a slash, to link two or more words which together modify a following word, where the words linked do not form a compound, as in:**

  the space–time continuum

  a 45–15 win for the British Lions

  a derailment on the Glasgow–Edinburgh line

  a France–Croatia final

  While is it often the case that a hyphen is used for constructions of this type, especially in handwritten texts, it is preferable – where this is possible – to use a short dash if the words linked do not form a compound. For hyphens in compound words, see the next chapter.

The slash

The slash (/) is also called the oblique, the solidus, the stroke or the virgule.

It has five main uses:

- **to separate alternatives, as in:**

  Dear Sir/Madam

  Each boy should bring a cup/mug, cutlery, pyjamas, a change of clothes, and three pairs of shoes and/or trainers.

  The athletes will each have his/her own room in the Olympic village. When s/he has finished his/her particular event or training for the day, he/she will have privacy and a place to relax.

- **to indicate an abbreviated form, as in:**

  Replies should be sent to Fraser Hamilton, c/o [= **care of**] Brown, 47 Appleyard Drive, Oxford.

- **to indicate a period of time, as in:**

  This assessment applies to the 1997/98 tax year.

  He has announced that he will retire at the end of the 1998/99 season.

- **to express rates and ratios, as in:**

  a top speed of 250 km/hr [= 250 kilometres per hour]

- **to link items, especially places on a route, as in:**

  The Edinburgh/Amsterdam/Frankfurt flight has been cancelled.

  Notice that here the slashes can be replaced by short dashes, but not hyphens.

A more recent, and increasingly familiar, use of the slash is as a specifier in the addresses for sites on the World Wide Web.

11

The hyphen

The **hyphen** (-) is the short line (shorter, that is, than the short dash discussed in the previous chapter) used to link words or parts of words to show that they are to be read as a single unit. A hyphen, unlike a dash, never has a space between it and a preceding or following letter.

There often seems to be little logic or consistency in the hyphenation of words in English. The reason for this is that there are few 'rules' as such – hyphenation is often more a question of style and common sense, rather than principle. Modern usage is characterized by the tendency to use a hyphen only when it is strictly necessary, with the result that texts have much less hyphenation than was hitherto the case. A text peppered with unnecessary hyphens can look both fussy and old-fashioned, and provided the few rules that do exist are adhered to, it is both desirable and correct to avoid hyphens wherever possible.

When is a hyphen necessary?

There are a couple of immutable rules that ought to be dealt with before coming to more specific examples.

The first and most important of these general rules is that a hyphen is essential when clarity demands it. Keep in mind that the only way that we can indicate in writing the stress patterns used in speech is to use appropriate punctuation. Hyphenation has an important role in this respect. Compare the following examples:

He has twenty-odd cousins.

He has twenty odd cousins.

If the intended sense here is 'He has twenty or more cousins' rather than 'He has twenty cousins who are peculiar in some way', the hyphen cannot be omitted.

When a compound word regarded as a single unit of meaning is made up of more than two words, and where the individual words within the compound belong to different word classes, hyphens are usually the only way that the words may be linked effectively, as in:

a will-o'-the-wisp ❑ a johnny-come-lately ❑ a ne'er-do-well

Here, it is obviously not possible to make a single word out of the elements of the phrase. Furthermore, if the words are not connected by hyphens it would make these phrases more difficult to read when they appear in context:

Karl was a johnny come lately to the joys of family life.

As is discussed in more detail later, the same principle applies to phrases made up of two or more words, when they are used adjectivally and come before a noun, as in:

a happy-go-lucky character ❑ an over-familiar approach ❑ a well-kept garden

The second important rule is that a hyphen must be used where a word is split at the end of a line. This use of the hyphen is common in printed texts and is illustrated in the following example:

He has often encountered a great deal of determined oppos-
ition from local residents.

ⓘ For word splits at the ends of lines, it is important to remember that the hyphen should always appear at the end of the first line, and never at the beginning of the second.

Where possible, it is better to avoid splitting words at the ends of lines, but when this is unavoidable the split should be made in a way that causes minimum interruption to the flow of the text. The following are some do's and don'ts on splitting words at the ends of lines:

Don't split words of five or fewer letters.

Do try to split longer words at a syllable break. The word should, ideally, be split somewhere in the middle so that it is more or less equally divided between the first and second line.

Do split words to avoid the possibility that the word may be mispronounced or read as a whole word on the first line.

Don't split a word in any way that may cause the reader to hesitate or re-read the split word in order to follow the sense.

Don't split words that already have a hyphen anywhere other than at that hyphen.

If you are in any doubt about where any word ought to be split, many ordinary dictionaries indicate where syllable breaks occur in words, and there are also specialist dictionaries dealing with spelling and word division.

Hyphens linking three or more words

As has been outlined above, multi-word phrases that function as nouns are usually hyphenated, as in the following examples:

> My brother-in-law is a barrister.
>
> The common name of this plant is love-lies-bleeding.
>
> She said she was fed up having to wear her sister's hand-me-downs.
>
> He popped up suddenly and alarmingly, like a jack-in-the-box.

In addition, and to avoid any ambiguity, multi-word phrases that describe a following noun are also hyphenated, as in:

> The balance-of-payments deficit has increased alarmingly.
>
> He expressed his reservations about what he described as too-good-to-be-true figures.
>
> She has that butter-won't-melt-in-my-mouth expression.
>
> The best advice I can give is that you steer a middle-of-the-road course.
>
> The paramedics tried mouth-to-mouth resuscitation and heart massage, to no avail.
>
> a lighter-than-air sponge cake

Notice that when phrases like this follow the noun, they are not hyphenated, as in:

> He reckons that the figures are too good to be true.
>
> The deficit in the balance of payments has increased alarmingly.

A hyphen linking two words

One of the commonest faults concerning hyphenation is the habit of unnecessarily adding a hyphen in phrases and two-word nouns whose meaning is perfectly clear without a hyphen. Here are some examples of phrases that should not be hyphenated:

> false teeth ❑ a fashion victim ❑ a mortise lock ❑ a putting green ❑ a root vegetable ❑ a violin concerto ❑ a plumber's mate

Hyphens are also often unnecessary in composite nouns, though more traditional writers may continue to use hyphens in words like *gate-keeper* and *book-seller* even when there is no good reason to do so. The joining of two words into a composite noun without a hyphen is a process that usually begins with the words being hyphenated, and, provided that there is no visually unacceptable juxtaposition of letters, or misreading that might result from making the hyphenated compound into a single word, the hyphen is gradually dropped. Thus, *seafood* and *seafront* have become single words, but *sea anemone* and *sea air* are written as two words because of the juxtaposition of vowels. *Moonflower* is written as one word, but *moon-eye* retains its hyphen because as *mooneye* it might be misread.

Two-word modifiers that precede the noun are always hyphenated so that the meaning is absolutely clear, as in the following examples:

> a subtle grey-green shade ❑ a pitch-dark night ❑ a well-developed instinct for survival ❑ the much-maligned policy ❑ one of the better-organized events ❑ a half-baked excuse ❑ a first-class ticket ❑ a long-standing feud

Notice that when intensifying words like 'well', 'better', 'best', 'ill', 'worse' and 'worst' are used with an adjective that follows the noun, the hyphen is often dropped, as in:

> His instinct for survival was particularly well developed.
>
> The event was better organized than most.

When an adverb ending in *-ly* and an adjective or other modifier precede the noun, there is usually no hyphen between the adverb and adjective, as in:

> a beautifully kept garden ❑ a greatly enlarged illustration ❑ abnormally sensitive gums ❑ he and his equally snobbish wife

However, when the *-ly* adverb + adjective or other modifier are considered to be so closely linked that they function as a single unit of meaning, a hyphen is sometimes added, as in:

> a mentally-handicapped child

tightly-packed spectators
slowly-moving traffic

Hyphens with prefixes

By and large, words that are formed using prefixes are written as single words without hyphens, thus *cooperate*, *multifarious*, *miniskirt*, *polytechnic*, *unable*.

However, when the addition of a prefix would create confusion with another word, a hyphen is often inserted to make the meaning clear. Thus *re-creation* meaning 'the act of creating again' is distinguished from *recreation* meaning 'a relaxing or enjoyable activity', and *re-cover* meaning 'to cover again' is distinguished from *recover* meaning 'to get (something) back or to regain one's health'. Similarly, if the addition of the prefix without a hyphen produces a difficult-to-read juxtaposition of letters, a hyphen is required. Thus, write *non-nuclear* rather than *nonnuclear* and *pre-empt* rather than *preempt*.

When a prefix is added to a hyphenated compound, a hyphen must also be added between the prefix and the first word of the compound, as in:

his pre-university-lecturing days

A hyphen is also required when the first letter of the word to which the prefix is attached has a capital letter, as in:

anti-American ❑ a non-Christian ❑ pre-Chaucer

12

Capital letters

This chapter offers some guidance on the use of capital letters, even though, strictly speaking, the capitalization of words is not part of punctuation.

Full sentences and sentence fragments

As has been discussed in earlier chapters, ordinary sentences begin with a capital letter. This also applies to so-called sentence fragments.

Here are some full sentences and sentence fragments with initial capitals:

> She was running the hamburger stall, and I don't think she has ever worked so hard in her life.
>
> A good dictionary is an invaluable aid for students, no matter what they happen to be studying.
>
> Will he ever be able to find a decent job? Somehow, I doubt it.
>
> I have to find five hundred dollars before next week. No chance!

Proper names

A capital is used for the first letter of proper names: that is, for the names of people and places. Here are some examples:

> Paul ❑ William ❑ Donald Macpherson ❑ Anne Ross ❑ Asia ❑ Mexico ❑ Poland ❑ St Kitts and Nevis ❑ Sussex ❑ Kuala Lumpur ❑ Lake Winnipeg ❑ Ben Nevis ❑ the Pacific Ocean ❑ the Southern Uplands ❑ the Pennine Way ❑ the Great North Road ❑ Mars ❑ the Milky Way

Capitals are used for the titles of books, plays, films, newspapers, etc. When the title is made up of several words, it is usually only the most important words that are given capitals, unless an unimportant word such as an indefinite or definite article is the first word of the title. Here are some examples:

Three Men in a Boat ❑ The Merchant of Venice ❑ The Man that would be King ❑ The Sunday Times

In the same way, capitals are used for each important element in the official titles of people, institutions, organizations, buildings, etc. Here are some examples:

His Royal Highness, the Prince of Wales ❑ William the Conquerer ❑ the Duke of Buccleuch ❑ the Foreign Secretary ❑ the Archbishop of Canterbury ❑ the Pope ❑ the House of Lords ❑ the Church of Ireland ❑ the Inland Revenue ❑ the Academy of Dramatic Arts ❑ the Department of Trade and Industry ❑ the Clyde Port Authority ❑ Westminster Abbey ❑ the Tower of London ❑ the Sears Building ❑ the White House.

Note that when a title has been shortened but refers to a specific person or institution, the capital is retained, as in:

the Duke and his wife ❑ the Commons ❑ the Revenue

But, when the title is used in a more general way and does not therefore refer to a specific individual, it can – and usually is – written without a capital, as in:

the dukes of Lorraine ❑ the prime ministers of France and Spain ❑ successive popes

He hopes to be a junior vice-president by the time he's thirty.

Words derived from proper names

In general, words that are derived from proper names also have an initial capital letter, as in:

the Scottish parliament ❑ the Napoleonic system ❑ the Brazilian national squad ❑ Victorian architecture ❑ the Cyrillic alphabet ❑ Shakespearean tragedies

Included in this category are many two-word compounds that include a proper name or an adjective denoting a country or region. These are also written with a capital letter:

Brussels lace ❑ French leave ❑ Cornish pasty ❑ Lancashire hotpot ❑ Irish moss

But, for some compounds, the word which names or is derived from the name of a country or region may equally correctly be written with or without a capital letter:

brussels/Brussels sprouts ▫ plaster of paris/Paris ▫ a danish/Danish pastry

Some of these compounds are always written without a capital:

venetian blinds ▫ arabic numerals ▫ roman type

Certain words derived from proper names never take a capital letter. These include things that were originally named after a particular person or place, but are no longer directly associated with that person or place, as in:

pasteurize (after Louis *Pasteur*) ▫ guillotine (after Joseph-Ignace *Guillotin*) ▫ spoonerism (after Rev W A *Spooner*) ▫ wellington (after the 1st Duke of *Wellington*) ▫ sandwich (after John Montagu, 4th Earl of *Sandwich*) ▫ strontium (after *Strontian*, a village in Argyllshire) ▫ ampere (from André Marie *Ampère*)

The names of days of the week, months and festivals start with a capital letter.

Friday the thirteenth ▫ Good Friday ▫ He'll be fifteen in March ▫ Easter Sunday ▫ Diwali or the Festival of Lights

Notice that the seasons 'summer', 'autumn' and 'winter' do not require a capital letter, but that 'spring' may have a capital to distinguish it from the other senses of the word, as in:

He had a spring in his step, and Spring was in the air.

The names of languages and their related adjectives start with a capital.

He's studying French, Italian, Latin and Greek. ▫ a Spanish phrasebook ▫ They speak Urdu at home.

In published writing, all brand names and trademarks mentioned should have a capital letter, even where the brand name has come to be used generically for a whole class of similar products, as is the case with *Hoover®*, *Sellotape®* and *Xerox®*. If a capital letter is not used, legal action may be taken by the manufacturer of the product. However, when the brand name is used as a verb, no capital letter is necessary, as in:

Have you hoovered the bedrooms yet?

I've sellotaped a note to the door.

➤ For the use of capitals in abbreviations see Chapter 13.

13

Abbreviations

Abbreviations are shortened forms of words or phrases. They are used principally to save space in writing, but they are also commonly used in speech when people want to avoid using a long or complicated title or name. An abbreviation often becomes so widely used that it is more familiar than the full form: the abbreviation MP is used as much, and probably more than, the full form 'member of parliament'; and, TUC is as familiar and as readily understood by British people as 'Trades Union Congress'.

An important point to remember as far as punctuation is concerned: when an abbreviation with a full stop after its last letter comes at the end of a sentence, there is no need to write another full stop:

> He usually leaves for work around 7 a.m.

In American texts there is generally greater use of full stops in abbreviations than in modern British texts. Modern British style tends towards minimum punctuation and this includes the punctuation of most types of abbreviation: for example, the abbreviation for Doctor of Literature would usually be written D.Lit. in American texts and DLit in British texts.

There are four types of abbreviation.

Part-word abbreviations

A part-word abbreviation is a shortened form in which part of the word is written in place of the whole word. Part-word abbreviations are usually (but not always) followed by a full stop. Abbreviations of this type should, in general, be avoided in formal writing. They are, however, perfectly acceptable in less formal contexts, such as e-mail, and in certain specialized texts where space is at a premium. Examples include:

Prof. [= Professor]
Wed. [= Wednesday]
Oct. [= October]
approx. [= approximately]
fem. [= feminine]
derog. [= derogatory]

Abbreviated forms of measurements, eg cm [= centimetre(s)] and kg [= kilogram(s)] should, in general, be confined to technical and scientific contexts. Most abbreviations for measurements have no full stops. Again, in normal prose and formal writing, words for measurements should be written out in full – it is considered bad style to use the abbreviated forms.

Contractions

Contractions are shortened forms that include the first and last letter of the word being shortened. Abbreviations of this type are used for conventional titles used with names in letter writing, and in writing addresses. Examples include:

Mr [= Mister]
Dr [= Doctor]
St [= Saint]
Rd. or Rd [= Road]
Ave. or Ave [= Avenue]
Gk [= Greek]
sthg [= something]
contd. or contd [= continued]
do. or do [= ditto]

Contractions follow the form of the whole word – if the whole word starts with a capital letter, the contraction also starts with a capital letter. A full stop at the end of the contraction is optional. However, modern British usage generally prefers no full stop, unless its absence would lead to a misreading of the contraction. In e-mail and electronic messaging, contracted forms of familiar or frequently occurring words are common and, almost without exception, have no full stops.

The contractions listed above only appear in writing. They are unpronounceable as short forms and are read and pronounced as the full form would be, so that *Mr* is read and pronounced *Mister*,

St is read and pronounced *Saint*, and so on.

Those contractions in which the missing letter or letters is/are replaced by apostrophes, and are pronounced as words in their own right, are discussed in Chapter 4.

Initialisms

Initialisms are abbreviations consisting of the first letter of each word in a group of words. They are distinct from acronyms in that each letter is pronounced separately.

When the initialism is the name of a country or organization, each letter of the initialism is written as a capital letter, as in UK, USA, USSR, UAE [= United Arab Emirates], BMA [= British Medical Association], and QPR [= Queens Park Rangers]. In some abbreviated forms of organizations, the word 'of' is also part of the initialism. This is usually written as a lower case *o*, as in DoE [= Department of the Environment] and FoE [= Friends of the Earth].

Note that when more than one letter from a word is taken into the abbreviation the second and subsequent letters are usually in lower case, as in BEng [= Bachelor of Engineering], BSc [= Bachelor of Science], and RAeS [= Royal Aeronautic Society] .

Other initialisms are usually written with all their letters in lower case, eg plc [= public limited company], aka [= also known as] and asap [= as soon as possible]. However, many of the new initialisms created for and used in e-mail and electronic messaging are typed in capitals even though they come from lower case full forms, eg BTW [= by the way], WRT [= with regard to], and AFAIK [= as far as I know].

In the past, most initialisms were written with full stops after each letter, but modern style prefers no full stops.

Here are some more examples:

BBC [= British Broadcasting Corporation]

CET [= Central European Time]

EU [= European Union]

RSPCA [= Royal Society for the Prevention of Cruelty to Animals]

UN [= United Nations]

GBH [= grievous bodily harm]

A-bomb [= atomic bomb]
GCSE [= General Certificate of Secondary Education]
IQ [= intelligence quotient]
R & R [= rest and recreation]
R & B [= rhythm and blues]
PC or pc [= personal computer]

The small number of initialisms that come from Latin phrases are written with lower case letters and have full stops. Increasingly, however, these abbreviations are written without full stops, though many people strongly disapprove of this practice.

Here are some examples:

a.m. or am [= ante meridiem]
p.m. or pm [= post meridiem]
e.g. or eg [= exempli gratia]
i.e. or ie [= id est]
c.f., cf. or cf [= confer]

Italic is often used in printed texts for abbreviated forms of Latin phrases and, when this style is adopted, full stops are usually omitted.

A word of warning about these Latin abbreviations – they are usually used inappropriately or punctuated wrongly. For this reason, it is generally best to avoid them in essay writing and other formal contexts and to recast the sentence or use an English equivalent.

Acronyms

Acronyms are abbreviations formed from the first letters of words in a phrase which, when combined, are pronounced as a new word.

All the letters in the acronym may be written as capitals – this is often the case for the titles of organizations or institutions, eg NATO and UNICEF.

Sometimes, acronyms are written with only the first letter capitalized, eg Aids [= acquired immune deficiency syndrome] and Benelux [= Belgium, Netherlands and Luxembourg].

A small number of acronyms have become more familiar than the full form of the phrase from which they come, with the acronyms being treated like ordinary words and written entirely in lower case letters, eg radar [= radio detecting and ranging], and scuba [= self-contained underwater breathing apparatus].

The following are more examples of acronyms:

ASH [= Action on Smoking and Health]

CAT scanner [= computer-aided (or -axial) tomography scanner]

SOGAT [= Society of Graphical and Allied Trades]

TESSA or Tessa [= tax exempt special saving account]

PEP or Pep [= personal equity plan]

Efta [= European Free Trade Association]

Asdic [= Anti-Submarine Detection Investigation Committee]

sonar [= sound navigation and ranging]

14

Diacritics and accents

What is a diacritic?

A diacritic is any mark above, below or sometimes through a letter, used to indicate that the letter is to be pronounced in a particular way. The term diacritic is used for all such marks, including accent marks. In written English, diacritics are usually only found in words that have been borrowed from other languages.

The following is a list of the more familiar diacritics from various languages:

acute accent	**é**	cedilla	**ç**
grave accent	**è**	tilde	**ñ**
circumflex accent	**â**	diaeresis or umlaut	**ü**

What is an accent?

An accent is a diacritic written or printed above a vowel, to show that the vowel is to be pronounced in a certain way, or that the vowel is stressed.

In French, accents usually indicate how a vowel is sounded. They are the acute accent (as in *née* and *blasé*), the grave accent (as in *à la*), and the circumflex accent (as in *raison d'être*).

The function of the acute accent in Spanish is to indicate stress. It appears over vowels that bear the main stress in a word, where this is contrary to the normal stress pattern of the language, as in *adiós*, *olé*, and *útil*. The tilde, over the letter *n*, indicates the 'ny' pronunciation, as in *señor*.

When you are citing a word from a foreign language, you should try to include any diacritical marks when you write the word. For handwritten work, this is easy enough to do. It is also possible to include the diacritics when you are using a word processor, either by typing a special numerical code for a particular mark or selecting it from a font display. The more sophisticated word processing programs have a spell-checking dictionary that includes many of the foreign words that have been absorbed into English, especially from French. Even if you type the word without the diacritic, the program will either correct it automatically or will prompt you to correct it.

Many words borrowed directly from foreign languages have become so well established in English that they are no longer considered to be foreign words at all and are never spelt with an accent (eg *hotel*, from the French *hôtel*). Other words and phrases are not fully naturalized in English and are always written with their accents. These include:

à la carte
à la mode
bête noire
cause célèbre
détente
déjà vu
Führer
idée fixe
maître d'hôtel
mañana
pièce de résistance
précis
raison d'être
señorita
tête-à-tête

Many French words are at an intermediary stage in the process of naturalization into English, and for these use of the accent is now considered to be optional. In the following list, the more usual form is shown first:

après-ski *or* apres-ski
clientele *or* clientèle
debris *or* débris
debut *or* début
café *or* cafe
cortege *or* cortège
fête *or* fete
discotheque *or* discothèque
divorcee *or* divorcée
fiancee *or* fiancée
naive *or* naïve
née *or* nee
negligee *or* negligée
premiere *or* première
role *or* rôle
séance *or* seance
soiree *or* soirée

It is, however, better not to omit the diacritic in words where the accented letter would be pronounced differently, or not pronounced at all in English. Words in this category include:

attaché	manqué
blasé	passé
cliché	risqué
communiqué	soufflé
façade	soupçon
fiancé	

As has already been stated earlier in this chapter, diacritics are usually only used for foreign words. However, there are a couple of occasions where they are used in English words. A grave accent is occasionally used to show that the *e* in an *-ed* ending is pronounced as a separate letter, as in *blessèd*, *learnèd* and *agèd*; and the diaeresis is sometimes printed over vowels for the same reason, as in *noël*.

15

Numbers, fractions and dates

This short chapter deals with the punctuation issues in writing numbers, fractions and dates in non-technical texts.

Numbers and fractions in formal writing

In formal texts, numbers from one to twenty should always be written out in full, ie as *one*, *two*, *fifteen*, and so on. Fractions should also be written out in full.

Also in formal texts, it is preferable to write out numbers from twenty-one to ninety-nine. Remember to include a hyphen when you are writing out fractions and compound numbers in the range from twenty-one to ninety-nine, thus: *three-quarters*, *five-eighths*, *twenty-one*, *forty-four*, *ninety-seven*. Note, however, there is no hyphen in larger compound numbers: 323 is written out as *three hundred and twenty-three* (not *three-hundred-and-twenty-three*).

It is quite acceptable to write larger numbers using digits, especially where the full written form would produce a cumbersome appearance. However, if a sentence starts with a number, the number should always be written out in full, or, if you have been using digits for other large numbers within the same text, the sentence should be recast so that the number does not come at the beginning of the sentence.

Here are some examples illustrating the various ways that numbers can or cannot be written in formal texts:

✗ She has 6 children, 10 grandchildren, and 14 great-grandchildren.

✓ She has six children, ten grandchildren, and fourteen great-grandchildren.

✓ The majority of the population is made up of people between the ages of forty-five and eighty-nine.

✓ The majority of the population is made up of people between the ages of 45 and 89.

✓ Nearly a quarter of these children are seriously undernourished.

✗ Nearly $\frac{1}{4}$ of these children are seriously undernourished.

✓ There are four hundred and twenty-three words in this column.

✗ There are four-hundred-and-twenty-three words in this column.

✓ There are 423 words in this column.

✓ At the last count, the combined population of the three villages was less than two thousand and fifty.

✓ At the last count, the combined population of the three villages was less than 2050.

✗ 750 people turned up for the rally.

✓ Seven hundred and fifty people turned up for the rally.

✓ The rally was attended by 750 people.

When a sentence contains an address, the street or building number is written as it would be on a letter or envelope, ie in numerals, whether or not it is a small or large number:

You might also want to visit the National Postal Museum at 2 Massachusetts Avenue, Washington DC.

Except for certain dates, pairs of numbers separated by a dash should include all the figures in each number. The second number should not be abbreviated:

✓ 253–255 cm

✗ 253–5 cm

➤ For date ranges see below.

Commas in numbers

In British printed texts, four-figure numbers are usually printed with no spaces between the digits, and no comma. Numbers with five or more digits are printed either with **thin spaces** (also called

hair spaces) or commas before every three digits counting from the right, like this:

14 575 or 14,575

2 753 000 or 2,753,000

American style prefers commas rather than thin spaces in printed texts.

In handwritten texts, where it is not possible to use a thin space, numbers with five or more digits should be written with commas before every three digits counting from the right. There is no need to use a comma in numbers from 1000 to 9999.

Dates

The commonest way of writing dates nowadays is in the order (number for the) day of the month + name of the month + (number for the) year. This is certainly the preferred style in most formal and business correspondence. It is no longer obligatory or even necessary to add commas between the elements. The following examples are all equally acceptable from the point of view of punctuation:

The standard was raised at Glenfinnan in April 1745.

The standard was raised at Glenfinnan in April, 1745.

On 16 April 1746, the final battle of the Jabobite rebellion took place at Culloden Moor in Invernesshire.

On 16 April, 1746, the final battle of the Jabobite rebellion took place at Culloden Moor in Invernesshire.

Bonnie Prince Charlie's Highland army was finally defeated at Culloden on April 16 1746.

Bonnie Prince Charlie's Highland army was finally defeated at Culloden on April 16, 1746.

It is also possible to write dates using figures for all the elements, as in *12/7/99*. However, it is best to be aware, especially if you are corresponding with Americans or others who use the American system, that this way of writing the date can cause confusion. In America 12/7/99 means '7 December 1999', while in Britain it means '12 July 1999'.

For periods of time, the paired elements can be linked either by a short dash or the words 'to' or 'and'. Remember that is it incorrect to use a dash if the first year is preceded by a preposition:

✓ 15–25 June 1999

✓ 1999–2005

✗ from 15–25 June 1999

✓ from 15th to 25th June 1999

✗ between 1999–2005

✓ between 1999 and 2005

When you use a dash to link years or other periods of time in this way, it is common practice to use the fewest number of digits possible. Thus: *1902–5*, *1915–18*, *1932–5*. However, when the range includes two different centuries, all the figures must be written, as in: *1999–2005*.

Sometimes a year is written with the abbreviation AD or BC. In printed texts, these abbreviations are usually in small capitals, rather than ordinary capitals. AD is usually written before the year, eg *AD 1003*. BC is written after the year, as in: *274 BC*. To avoid misinterpretation, it is important to remember that pairs of years with the abbreviation BC should include all the figures for both years, as in: *251–224 BC*. If this range was written as *251–24 BC*, it would be indistinguishable from *251 BC–24 BC*.

16

Miscellaneous

Accurate punctuation is only one of the things that you have to think about when you are producing written work.

The general appearance of the text is also an important consideration and in this chapter, some guidance is given on this aspect of writing.

The uses of italic and bold type are discussed, amongst other things, in the section on printed texts.

Presentation and layout

Whether you are writing an essay, a report or a business letter, it is always a good idea to spend some time thinking about the presentation and layout of your writing.

A rough outline or draft is a good way to start – you can summarize and organize the main points that you want to cover. Next organize the information into paragraphs. Each paragraph should contain one key point, and all the sentences in the paragraph should contribute to or relate to this key point. When you move on to another point, begin a new paragraph.

Try to keep each paragraph short. If a paragraph is very long, check to see if it contains more than one key point, each of which could be made the core of a separate paragraph. On the other hand, check that there is at least one key point in every paragraph: any paragraph that does not include a separate point should be combined with the preceding or following one.

Make sure sentences are not so long or complicated that they obscure the meaning of what you are trying to say. If there is a risk that the reader may lose track of what is being said, split the sentence into smaller parts.

Check the grammar, spelling and punctuation. Check, in particular, the use of paired punctuation marks: a common error is to put an opening bracket, comma or dash at the beginning of an inserted comment, and then to forget the closing bracket, or the second comma or dash. Check also that each element of the pair is in the correct position in the sentence.

When writing a business letter, make sure that what you write is brief, courteous, accurate and to the point. The most widely used layout for business letters is the fully blocked style with open punctuation. This means that all paragraphs and headings are set against the left-hand margin (with no indents for new paragraphs), and that punctuation is kept to the minimum required for clarity. If you are using a letterhead leave a two-line space before typing the date. No punctuation is required in the date. After the date, type the name and address of the person the letter is being sent to. Again, no punctuation is needed at the ends of the lines in the address.

Printed texts

Many people now have, or have access to, a personal computer with a word-processing program. These programs are becoming increasingly sophisticated year by year, and it is now perfectly possible for anyone to create professional-looking documents that would, in the past, have required the services of a specialist printer. Some word processors allow you to choose from various layouts for different types of document, such as business letters, memos and even CVs.

Word processors can also produce italic and bold type.

Italics

Italics are letters that slope to the right, like this: *italic letters*.

In printed texts, italics are used in the following ways:

- The titles of books, plays, films, newspapers and works of art are italicized. So too are the titles of musical works, provided they have a special title, and are not simply known by a number and the musical form in which they have been written. As has already been mentioned in the chapter on quotes, the titles of poems that form part of a collection or anthology are not normally italicized. However, when a long poem is published as a volume in its own right, italics are used when printing its title. Finally, the names used in legal cases are usually written in italics. Here are some examples:

George Elliot's *Middlemarch*

Waiting for Godot by Samuel Beckett

The popular western *The Magnificent Seven* was based on Kurosawa's 1954 film *Seven Samurai*.

the *Washington Post*

Picasso's *Guernica*

Mozart's Symphony No. 41 in D major, *Jupiter*

the Old English heroic poem *Beowulf*

Chapman v *Penderley* [Note that the 'v' is not printed in italic]

- The names of ships, aircraft and spacecraft are also italicized, as in:

  The Japanese battleships, *Musashi* and *Yumato*, two of the largest ever built, were both sunk in World War II.

  the airship *Hindenburg*

  Neil Armstrong and Buzz Aldrin landed on the Moon in the spacecraft *Eagle*.

- Italics are sometimes used to draw attention to a word or words that the writer wants to emphasize, as in:

  'I *quite* agree.'

  'Make *him* do the washing-up for a change.'

- You can also use italics instead of inverted commas when you are talking about words:

  The words *wicked* and *sad* have acquired new meanings.

  Don't use *afflict* when you mean *inflict*.

- Foreign words and phrases that have not been naturalized into English are often printed in italics. This is also a convenient way of distinguishing any foreign word that has the same spelling as an English word.

  This was her particular *bête noire*.

  according to Kant's view of *a priori* cognition

  the concepts of *Gemeinschaft* and *Gesellschaft*

  a bottle of *sake*

- Biological genus and species names are printed in italic type, as in:

  The jaguar, *Panthera onca*, inhabits woodland and savannah close to water.

  The common foxglove, *Digitalis purpurea*, yields the drug digitalis, used to treat heart complaints.

Bold type

Bold type may be used for chapter headings and section headings. Bold type has been used in this way throughout this book. It can also be used as an alternative to italic when you want to highlight or emphasize a word. Again, this style has been used in places throughout this book.

E-mail

The style used in e-mail is generally much less formal than in other forms of correspondence. Punctuation is generally kept to a minimum, particularly in abbreviations and other shortened forms. Most e-mail messages are in what is known as plain text, like this:

```
I look forward to hearing from you.
```

Plain text uses capital letters and lower case letters, but not italics, bold type and underlining. Because it is more difficult to convey emotion or emphasis in the plain text format, some people use all capital letters for a word that they want to emphasize. Take care with this — capital letters are also used to convey anger — it may be misinterpreted.

17

American style

So far, this book has dealt mainly with the rules and conventions of punctuation as practised in British English. However, as has been signalled in passing references throughout the previous chapters, American style differs from British style in several important aspects. The British tend to use 'open punctuation', that is, minimum punctuation. The Americans, on the other hand, tend to be rather more conventional and strict in their approach.

The following compares the two styles and summarizes the main differences between them:

Full stops

For certain abbreviations, American style displays a more pronounced tendency to retain the full stops that the British regard as optional. Thus, the Americans prefer to keep full stops in abbreviations such as *eg* and *ie*.

See below for the position of the full stop in quoted material.

Commas

In lists of items, the Americans often use a comma after the item in the list that is immediately followed by a conjunction (*and* or *or*). More often that not, the British omit this final listing comma. Compare the following examples:

> Alice, Siobhan, and Liam will be coming to the party too.
> [= American style]
>
> Alice, Siobhan and Liam will be coming to the party too.
> [= British style]
>
> Are you going to have the fish, the salad, or the pasta?
> [= American style]

Are you going to have the fish, the salad or the pasta? [= British style]

Where there is continuity of subject between the clauses of a sentence that consists of two clauses connected by a linking word or words such as *and*, *because* and *in order*, the British regard a comma before the linking word as optional. American style prefers a comma before the linking word. Compare the following examples:

Malcolm is related to me by marriage, and is a regular house-guest. [= American style]

Malcolm is related to me by marriage and is a regular house-guest. [= British style]

Candida looked exhausted, because she had been travelling all night. [= American style]

Candida looked exhausted because she had been travelling all night. [= British style]

In American texts, numbers over 1000 have a comma after the first number. The British tend not to use commas in four-figure numbers, eg:

We estimate that the final figure will be between 1,300 and 2,500. [= American style]

We estimate that the final figure will be between 1300 and 2500. [= British style]

Quotation marks

In American style, double quotation marks are used to enclose a quotation, where British style prefers single quotes. For a quotation within a quotation Americans use single quotes within double quotes, where the British would use double quotes within single quotes.

Americans put commas and full stops inside the closing quotation mark whether or not the punctuation 'belongs' to the quoted material or not. Compare the following examples:

Shakespeare once said 'all the world's a stage.' [= American style]

Shakespeare once said 'all the world's a stage'. [= British style]

“At first she said ‘I don’t think I should,’ but then she said ‘Well, okay, just this once.’” [= American style]

‘At first she said “I don’t think I should”, but then she said “Well, okay, just this once”.’ [= British style]

18

Exercises

This chapter is devoted to a series of exercises that can be used to practise what has been learned in previous chapters of the book. There are eight sections with exercises that deal with each of the main punctuation marks in turn. Solutions to all these exercises can be found in the second section of this chapter.

Exercises

Exercise 1: Full stops

Try inserting full stops and capital letters in the following short passage. The commas are in the correct places, but all full stops and capital letters have been purposely omitted.

> beside herself with rage and humiliation, she paced the floor grinding her teeth she was so focussed on thoughts of revenge she didn't hear the door opening it wasn't until her mother was standing in her line of vision that she became aware that someone was actually witnessing her inarticulate mutterings and oaths she stopped in her tracks, suddenly more embarrassed than angry

Exercise 2: Full stops

The next passage has both clauses and sentences punctuated by commas. This makes it very difficult to read. For clarity's sake, it needs to be rewritten as a series of separate sentences using full stops and capital letters. It will help you to know that, correctly punctuated, the passage consists of **eight** separate sentences.

> We climbed and climbed, backs and calf muscles aching, we reached a narrow ridge where a cairn had been built, added to year by year and stone by stone by generations of walkers and climbers, sitting at the base were a family of four from

Leicester with their huge backpacks open on the ground, we greeted each other cheerfully and Jane and I sat down nearby, they offered us hot coffee from their flasks and delicious-looking rock buns, we accepted gratefully, if a little breathlessly, when we had caught our breath we told them it was the first hill we'd ever climbed, they didn't seem surprised.

Exercise 3: Questions marks and exclamations marks

Where should a question mark or exclamation mark be inserted in these sentences? Is one or either required in every case?

When will we see you again

'Do you actually like oysters' Bob enquired.

Was it Peter or Harry who asked 'Will we be paid expenses'

The question that immediately comes to mind on reading the report is why this problem was not identified earlier

Wow What a glorious sunset

'Stop making that horrible noise immediately' she bellowed.

Exercise 4: Apostrophes

Here are some sentences with words that have apostrophes missing. Take care to add an apostrophe only to those words that should have one.

Its time we put the budgie back in its cage.

Theyll get back home at about one oclock in the morning our time.

I couldnt brake quickly enough and now my sons bike has a buckled front wheel.

Its all curled up into a ball so you cant see its head.

Isnt this anyones newpaper? If it isnt, Ill take it home with me.

Ive been reading Keats poems.

Youll have to decide which is yours and which is hers.

Ones financial situation is surely ones own business?

Exercise 5: Apostrophes

Try making the following phrases possessive using an apostrophe or an apostrophe + *s*.

the house of my father	my father's house

the workshop of the blacksmith ....
the children of the Smiths ....
the toys of the children ....
the masts of the boats ....
the surgery of Dr Charles ....
the rear wheel of the Mercedes ....

Exercise 6: Commas

Here are some sentences that have no commas between the capital letter at the beginning and the full stop at the end. Do you know where the commas should go?

It was the longest most boring journey I've ever had to endure.

He had a big lump on his head a fractured wrist a bruise on his cheek and a small cut above his right eye.

The driver braked violently and flinging open the car door jumped out and grabbed the boy by the collar.

Even in 1950 however beer production was largely regional if not local and there were still some 310 firms with 540 separate breweries.

As the train pulled into the station heads popped out of every window.

Hey Harry have you got a moment?

Clumsily like a fallen horse righting itself she scrambled to her feet gathered up the bananas marshmallows umbrella thermos handbag and other possessions that had fallen or rolled around her and waving reassuringly walked briskly away.

Exercise 7: Colons

Where should a colon be inserted in these sentences, and where is a comma also needed?

Here is the fruit you asked me to get a pound of grapes four oranges and half a dozen bananas.

The Life of Oscar Wilde Tragedy or Farce?

I'm sure I've packed everything suntan lotion swimwear mosquito repellent film for the camera passports and money.

Exercise 8: Semicolons

Here are some sentences in which it might be appropriate to use a semicolon. There are missing commas and full stops in these sentences too. Where can a semicolon be used, and where should other punctuation marks go?

Dickens is my favourite author Trollope is a close second

You shouldn't regard this as a setback see it instead as a pause for reflection

The country's wealth was built on the more traditional industries of steel-making shipbuilding and heavy engineering textiles clothing and carpet manufacture pottery and glass-making and coal-mining

In order to meet the criteria for inclusion in the common European currency both France and Italy have had to take steps to reduce government spending consequently the unemployment rate in both countries has risen significantly

Exercise 9: Quotation marks

The following sentences should have some part enclosed in quotation marks. The punctuation that ought to come before or after the quotation marks has also been omitted.

It was in this film that the character played by Michael Douglas famously said lunch is for wimps

Be careful walking on these pavements children Frankie warned because they're covered with black ice

Why don't you do a search on the Internet asked his teacher you might find something that would be helpful to you

Who shouted Watch out

Next week we'll examine the stream of consciousness technique in greater detail the tutor announced

They spoke a very archaic form of English full of thous and thees

It's interesting to note how the meanings of the words sad and wicked have changed in recent years

Exercise 10: Brackets and dashes

These sentences each contain a short parenthetical phrase that may be enclosed by either a pair of round brackets or a pair of dashes. Note that there may also be missing commas in some of

the sentences.

A majority of those polled on Tuesday and Wednesday 55% and 57% respectively do not believe the president should resign.

Josh or Nick I'm not sure which will pick you up from the station tomorrow.

In his attempt to secure the succession for his strongly Protestant daughter-in-law Warwick now duke of Northumberland failed dismally.

We know Mr Weller we who are men of the world that a good uniform must work its way with the women sooner or later.

19

Solutions to exercises

Exercise 1: Full stops

Beside herself with rage and humiliation, she paced the floor grinding her teeth. She was so focussed on thoughts of revenge she didn't hear the door opening. It wasn't until her mother was standing in her line of vision that she became aware that someone was actually witnessing her inarticulate mutterings and oaths. She stopped in her tracks, suddenly more embarrassed than angry.

Exercise 2: Full stops

We climbed and climbed, backs and calf muscles aching. We reached a narrow ridge where a cairn had been built, added to year by year and stone by stone by generations of walkers and climbers. Sitting at the base were a family of four from Leicester with their huge backpacks open on the ground. We greeted each other cheerfully and Jane and I sat down nearby. They offered us hot coffee from their flasks and delicious-looking rock buns. We accepted gratefully, if a little breathlessly. When we had caught our breath we told them it was the first hill we'd ever climbed. They didn't seem surprised.

Exercise 3: Question marks and exclamation marks

When will we see you again?

'Do you actually like oysters?' Bob enquired.

Was it Peter or Harry who asked 'Will we be paid expenses?' [*Note*: *the question mark can also be moved so that it is outside the final quotation mark because the whole sentence is also a question*]

The question that immediately comes to mind on reading the report is why this problem was not identified earlier.

[*Note: this is an indirect question so should be punctuated with a full stop*]

Wow! What a glorious sunset!

'Stop making that horrible noise immediately!' she bellowed.

Exercise 4: Apostrophes

It's time we put the budgie back in its cage.

They'll get back home at about one o'clock in the morning our time.

I couldn't brake quickly enough and now my son's bike has a buckled front wheel.

It's all curled up into a ball so you can't see its head.

Isn't this anyone's newpaper? If it isn't, I'll take it home with me.

I've been reading Keats' poems.

You'll have to decide which is yours and which is hers.

One's financial situation is surely one's own business?

Exercise 5: Apostrophes

the house of my father	my father's house
the workshop of the blacksmith	the blacksmith's work-shop
the children of the Smiths	the Smiths' children
the toys of the children	the children's toys
the masts of the boats	the boats' masts
the surgery of Dr Charles	Dr Charles's surgery *or* Dr Charles' surgery
the rear wheel of the Mercedes	the Mercedes' rear wheel

Exercise 6: Commas

It was the longest, most boring journey I've ever had to endure.

He had a big lump on his head, a fractured wrist, a bruise on his cheek, and a small cut above his right eye.

The driver braked violently, and flinging open the car door, jumped out and grabbed the boy by the collar.

Even in 1950, however, beer production was largely regional, if not local, and there were still some 310 firms with 540 separate breweries.

As the train pulled into the station, heads popped out of every window.

Hey, Harry, have you got a moment?

Clumsily, like a fallen horse righting itself, she scrambled to her feet, gathered up the bananas, marshmallows, umbrella, thermos, handbag, and other possessions that had fallen or rolled around her, and, waving reassuringly, walked briskly away.

Exercise 7: Colons

Here is the fruit you asked me to get: a pound of grapes, four oranges and half a dozen bananas.

The Life of Oscar Wilde: Tragedy or Farce?

I'm sure I've packed everything: suntan lotion, swimwear, mosquito repellent, film for the camera, passports and money.

Exercise 8: Semicolons

Dickens is my favourite author; Trollope is a close second.

You shouldn't regard this as a setback; see it instead as a pause for reflection.

The country's wealth was built on the more traditional industries of steel-making, shipbuilding and heavy engineering; textiles, clothing and carpet manufacture; pottery and glass-making; and coal-mining.

In order to meet the criteria for inclusion in the common European currency, both France and Italy have had to take steps to reduce government spending; consequently, the unemployment rate in both countries has risen significantly.

Exercise 9: Quotation marks

It was in this film that the character played by Michael Douglas famously said, 'Lunch is for wimps.'

'Be careful walking on these pavements, children,' Frankie warned, 'because they're covered with black ice.'

'Why don't you do a search on the Internet?' asked his teacher. 'You might find something that would be helpful to you.'

Who shouted, 'Watch out!'?

'Next week we'll examine the "stream of consciousness" technique in greater detail,' the tutor announced.

They spoke a very archaic form of English full of 'thous' and 'thees'.

It's interesting to note how the meanings of the words 'sad' and 'wicked' have changed in recent years.

Exercise 10: Brackets and dashes

A majority of those polled on Tuesday and Wednesday (55% and 57% respectively) do not believe the president should resign.

Josh or Nick (I'm not sure which) will pick you up from the station tomorrow.

In his attempt to secure the succession for his strongly Protestant daughter-in-law, Warwick—now duke of Northumberland—failed dismally.

We know, Mr Weller – we who are men of the world – that a good uniform must work its way with the women, sooner or later.

[*Note: the unspaced em dash and the spaced en dash are interchangeable in the last two sentences.*]

Index

abbreviations 59–63
acronyms 62
upper and lower case in 62
contractions 60–61
initialisms 61–62
from Latin 62
upper and lower case in 61
of measurements 60
part-word 59–60
used in e-mail 61
accents 64
functions of 64
optional use of 65
American style 75–77
commas in 75–76
full stops in 75
quotation marks in 76–77
apostrophe 12–16
in plurals 13
indicating possession 14–16
misuse of 12–13
bold type 74
brackets 41–45
angle 45
brace 45
round 41–44
enclosing an explanation 41
for a comment 42
for a reference 42
for abbreviations 42
for additional information 42
for an example 42
for identifying information 42
for saving space 43
for showing equivalents 42
when not to use 43
square 44
business letters: layout of 72
capital letters 56–58
at the beginning of sentences 56
in abbreviations 58
in brand names 58
in days of the week 58
in proper names 56–57
in words derived from proper names 57–58
colon 28–30
in direct speech and quotations 29–30
in memos 30
in ratios 30
in titles 30
preceding an explanation 28
comma 17–27
bracketing 20–22
in letter-writing 26–27

in lists of adjectives 19–20
in lists of nouns 18–19
indicating a pause 25
indicating omission 24–25
separating a main clause from a 'result' clause 23–24
separating a subordinate clause from a main clause 23
separating two main clauses 22–23
used to clarify meaning 24
when not to use 25–26

dash 46–49
long (em dash, em rule) 46–48
to avoid spelling in full 48
to enclose an explanation 47
to indicate curtailment 48
to indicate emphatic tone 47–48
to sum up what has gone before 47
short (en dash, en rule) 46–49
instead of slashes 49
to indicate ranges 48–49
to link words 49

dates 69
AD and BC 70
American style 69
commas in 69
ranges 70

diacritics 64

direct speech 4–5
colon in 29

e-mail 74

exclamation mark 9–11
avoidance of 10–11
in exclamatory questions 10
in imperatives 10
in quotations 10
or full stop 5
to show emotion 11
used to show emphasis 9
within parentheses 11

exclamation point. See **exclamation mark**

exercises 78–82

fractions 67
in formal writing 67

full point. See **full stop**

full stop 1–5
as a sentence marker 1–2
in direct speech 4–5
in partial sentences 3–4
or comma 2–3
over-use of 3
used to show omission 4

hyphen 51–55
for clarity 51
in compound words 52
in line-endings 52–53
in multi-word phrases 53
linking three or more words 53
linking two words 53–54
two-word modifiers 54–55
with prefixes 55

imperatives
exclamation mark in 10

interrogation mark. See **question mark**

inverted commas. See **quotation marks**

italics 72

numbers 67

commas in 68
in addresses 68
in formal writing 67
oblique. See **slash**
omission marks 4
paragraphs 71
parentheses. See **brackets, round**
period. See **full stop**
question mark 6–8
in direct questions 6–7
in indirect questions 7
in rhetorical questions 7
inside parentheses 8
or full stop 5
quotation marks 34–40
affecting other punctuation 36–38
within quotation marks 34
in direct quotations 34–36
in titles 39
problems with 39–40
single or double 34
to highlight a word 38
used in distancing 38–39
quotations
colon in 29
quotes. See **quotation marks**
semicolon 31–33
between clauses 31–32
in lists 32–33
slash 49–50
to express rates + ratios 50
to indicate a period of time 50
to indicate an abbreviation 49
to link items 50
to separate alternatives 49
solidus. See **slash**
solutions to exercises 83–86
stroke. See **slash**
virgule. See **slash**